3 MINUTES
with
Jesus

3 MINUTES
with
Jesus

180 Devotions for Women

JANICE THOMPSON

BARBOUR
PUBLISHING

Published by Barbour Publishing, Inc., 1810 Barbour Drive, Uhrichsville, Ohio 44683, www.barbourbooks.com

Our mission is to inspire the world with the life-changing message of the Bible.

Printed in China.

INTRODUCTION

The greatest gift that God ever gave this world was the gift of His Son, Jesus. If you know the Son, you know the Father.

These devotions will help you do just that. Here you will find inspiration and encouragement from God's Word meant to draw you closer to your Savior so that you can better know your heavenly Father. Within these pages, you'll be guided through just-right-size readings that you can experience in as few as three minutes:

- Minute 1: Reflect on God's Word
- Minute 2: Read real-life application and encouragement
- Minute 3: Pray

These devotions aren't meant to be a replacement for digging deep into the scriptures or for personal, in-depth quiet time. Instead, consider them a perfect jump-start to help you form a habit of spending time with God every day. Or add them to the time you're already spending with Him. May you come to a deeper relationship with Jesus as you read, apply, and pray.

JESUS, IMMANUEL (GOD WITH US)

*"So the Lord Himself will give you a special thing to see:
A young woman, who has never had a man, will give
birth to a son. She will give Him the name Immanuel."*

Isaiah 7:14 NLV

It must have been such a shock to the disciples to learn that Jesus—their friend—was God incarnate. "God with us" sounds great on paper, but having the author of the universe in the boat with you, fishing pole in hand? Those first few days must have been quite the trip!

Jesus came, God in flesh, to show us how loved and valued we are by our heavenly Father. He steps into our ordinary lives and transforms our thinking, our situations, and our hearts. His presence reminds us that God longs for personal relationship with His creation on good days and bad.

Thank You for coming in the flesh, Jesus. You stepped away from the magnificence of heaven and slipped into earthly sandals to plod along dusty roads with ordinary men and women like me. I'm so grateful for such overwhelming love. Amen.

JESUS, WONDERFUL COUNSELOR

For a child is born to us, a son is given to us. The government will rest on his shoulders. And he will be called: Wonderful Counselor, Mighty God, Everlasting Father, Prince of Peace.

ISAIAH 9:6 NLT

If you've ever been to a counselor or therapist, you know the value of having someone else to lean on. The expertise of the person in the chair across from you is a blessing, for sure, especially when you're feeling stuck.

Jesus is the best counselor of all. And talk about amazing advice! If you have a question, He has an answer. If you have a need, He has a solution. If you're feeling stuck, He's powerful (and gracious) enough to lift you from the quicksand and place your feet on solid ground.

The government of the world rests upon His shoulders. You can trust Him with your needs, no matter how great.

What an amazing counselor You are, Jesus. Today I come to You with the things I can't fix. Only You are capable, Lord, so I place my trust in You. Amen.

JESUS, FAMILIAR WITH GRIEF

He was despised and rejected—a man of sorrows, acquainted with deepest grief. We turned our backs on him and looked the other way. He was despised, and we did not care.

ISAIAH 53:3 NLT

When you're going through it—really going through it—you tend to gravitate to people who've walked a mile in your shoes. They "get" you when no one else does.

Today, if you're walking through a season of grief, remember. . .Jesus gets you. He was (and is) well acquainted with grief. Those who loved Him turned on Him. The people He came to save crucified Him. He knew the pain of separation from family and loved ones, and He also knew the pain of a broken heart.

He understands. He's been there. You can trust Him in your grief.

Jesus, I'm hurting today. The grief seems too much to bear. I come to You because I know You understand. Thank You for caring so much. Amen.

JESUS CARRIES OUR WEAKNESS

*Yet it was our weaknesses he carried; it was our sorrows
that weighed him down. And we thought his troubles were
a punishment from God, a punishment for his own sins!*

Isaiah 53:4 nlt

You're worn out. Exhausted. At the end of your rope. (Insert any cliché you like, and it's all the same—you're at the end of the end of your patience, energy, and want-to.)

What do you do when you're at that point of no return? Jesus hopes you'll turn to Him. When you can't carry it, He can. When you are sure there's not another ounce of power inside of you, He can energize you.

Jesus is the burden-lifter. He has super-human strength and can lift the things that have you weighted down today.

Take inventory. What feels too heavy to carry at this very moment? Hand it off to Him. He's right there, arms outstretched.

I give these burdens to You today, Jesus. I'm done! They're too much for me. Thank You for carrying them for me. Amen.

JESUS TOOK OUR PUNISHMENT

*But He was hurt for our wrong-doing. He was crushed
for our sins. He was punished so we would have
peace. He was beaten so we would be healed.*

ISAIAH 53:5 NLV

Picture a man headed to death row. He's been imprisoned for thirty years, and today is the day. He's earned the punishment with his crimes; now he must face the ultimate moment of truth.

Then, at the very last minute, a stranger steps in and says, "No, let me die in his place."

Picture the look of confusion on the faces of the guards. Imagine the shock and disbelief going on in the heart of the guilty one.

Friend, that's what Jesus did for you. When you least deserved it, He stepped in. He took your place. He said, "I'll cover this one because I love her."

He was crushed for our sins. He was punished so we would have peace. Oh, what a Savior, who loves us enough to die in our place!

---

*Thank You, Jesus, for the ultimate sacrifice—Your life on the cross.
You died for my sins. How can I ever thank You enough? Amen.*

JESUS, BORN IN A HUMBLE PLACE

*"Bethlehem Ephrathah, you are too little to be among
the family groups of Judah. But from you One will
come who will rule for Me in Israel. His coming
was planned long ago, from the beginning."*

MICAH 5:2 NLV

Maybe you've come from humble beginnings. You don't feel like
people view you as having much importance. That's okay! Jesus
came from humble beginnings too. He was born in a manger (an
animal stall) because there was no room for Him in the inn. There's
no mention in the Bible of Jesus owning His own home, wearing
fine clothes, or eating high-end foods.

He walked and talked with fishermen, prostitutes, tax collectors,
and other ordinary human beings just like you. His heart was
drawn to those who didn't meet the standards of society, those
who weren't viewed as valuable. And to those He said, "I find you
so valuable that I choose to lay down my life for you."

Don't despise your humble beginnings or wherever you might
be at this very moment. Jesus has been there, and He understands.

I'm so grateful You've walked a mile in my shoes, Jesus. Amen.

JESUS, THE HUMBLE KING

Rejoice, O people of Zion! Shout in triumph,
O people of Jerusalem! Look, your king is coming to
you. He is righteous and victorious, yet he is humble,
riding on a donkey—riding on a donkey's colt.
ZECHARIAH 9:9 NLT

When you think of royalty (or movie stars), you don't usually add the word *humble* to the description, do you? Most of those folks would be considered ostentatious, far from humble.

Jesus came as a babe in a manger, the lowest of the low. He was never the earthly king that people thought the Savior would be. (Boy, He really confused them all with that, didn't He?)

Even on the day He rode into town during the triumphal entry, Jesus came on the back of a donkey, the lowliest of beasts. He was saying to the people who adored Him, "I'm one of you."

Can you relate to that? Maybe you feel completely inadequate, insignificant. Rest assured, your status doesn't matter to Jesus. If anyone understands, He does.

Thank You for teaching me how to walk in humility,
Jesus! I want to be more like You. Amen.

JESUS, NAMED BY HIS FATHER

*"And she will have a son, and you are to name him
Jesus, for he will save his people from their sins."*
MATTHEW 1:21 NLT

How you ever talked to your parents about why they gave you the name they did? Sometimes, names are given for symbolic reasons. Other times, parents go out of their way to give unusual names so the child will feel unique.

When it came to Jesus, however, the name came straight from His father. Before He was ever born, the angel proclaimed the name: "You are to name Him Jesus."

Imagine Mary, still in shock over the news that she was pregnant by the Holy Spirit, now hearing that she didn't even get to name the baby! But God had a plan all along. Jesus means "Yahweh saves." Talk about prophetic! Before He ever arrived on the planet as a baby, Jesus was our salvation. What a glorious, heavenly name!

---

*Jesus, Your name is perfect! Thank You
for coming to save us all! Amen.*

JESUS, BORN OF A VIRGIN

"Look! The virgin will conceive a child!
She will give birth to a son, and they will call him
Immanuel, which means 'God is with us.' "

MATTHEW 1:22–23 NLT

There are so many miracles surrounding the life of Jesus that it's hard to pick one that stands out above the others. But perhaps the greatest—surely the most jaw-dropping—was the miracle of His birth.

Jesus was born to a virgin girl who had never been intimate with a man. The remarkable conception took place when the Spirit of God came upon her. And, as a young woman who had probably never traveled away from her parents, she went with Joseph, her betrothed, to Bethlehem. Alone. With no female family to help with the delivery. With no one to instruct her in the art of breastfeeding or holding and caring for a baby.

Jesus was born to a young woman who was completely innocent and inexperienced. But what an amazing mother she was!

Jesus, it astounds me that You were born of a
virgin. What a miracle Your birth was! Amen.

JESUS, THE GREAT FULFILLMENT

Then Jesus came from Galilee to the Jordan to John, to be baptized by him. John would have prevented him, saying, "I need to be baptized by you, and do you come to me?" But Jesus answered him, "Let it be so now, for thus it is fitting for us to fulfill all righteousness." Then he consented.

MATTHEW 3:13–15 ESV

Think of your favorite fairy tale. What if it had no ending? What if Cinderella never got the prince? What if Sleeping Beauty never awoke from her slumber?

A story without a happily-ever-after ending isn't very satisfying, is it?

Jesus was the perfect ending to mankind's sin story. He fulfilled the Law by becoming sin for us. On the day that His baptism took place, Jesus was saying to all of mankind, "It's fitting for me to wrap up this story. What was once broken and lost is now healed and found in me."

If Jesus hadn't come, if He hadn't submitted His life as a sacrifice for all, mankind's story would have ended badly. Aren't you grateful for a Savior who fulfilled your life story?

Thank You for coming, Jesus. Your sacrifice on the cross and resurrection from the grave were the perfect ending to our sin story. I'm so grateful for Your happily ever after! Amen.

JESUS, A PLEASURE TO HIS FATHER

And when Jesus was baptized, immediately he went up from
the water, and behold, the heavens were opened to him,
and he saw the Spirit of God descending like a dove and
coming to rest on him; and behold, a voice from heaven said,
"This is my beloved Son, with whom I am well pleased."
MATTHEW 3:16–17 ESV

Remember, as a child, how you loved to put a smile on Mom or
Dad's face? There was nothing better than making them laugh.
And when they gave you pats on the back, those were golden.
They kept you going.

You are like Jesus in that regard. His act of obedience (being
baptized by John) was enough to make His heavenly Father say,
"I'm proud of My boy!" That's what happens when we walk in
obedience. God looks down on us and says, "Great job, girl! I'm
so proud of you!"

Lord, I love the idea that I can put a smile on Your face. I'll be
more like Jesus. I'll obey and make Your heart glad! Amen.

JESUS, THE SPOKEN WORD

Jesus answered, "It is written: 'Man shall not live on bread alone, but on every word that comes from the mouth of God.' "

MATTHEW 4:4 NIV

We can't survive for long on food, can we? Eat a sandwich, and you're hungry again four or five hours later. Go to bed with a full stomach, and you wake up starving.

Jesus said it best: food won't get you there. If you really want to thrive, you need to learn to exist on the Word of God. Eat it like food. Memorize verses. Tape them to your refrigerator, your bathroom mirror. Keep them in your heart and your mind. They will sustain you long after that cheeseburger wears off.

You are the spoken Word, Jesus. You showed me how to live. Now I'll consume Your words so that I might have long life. Amen.

JESUS, A MESSAGE OF REPENTANCE

From that time on Jesus began to preach,
"Repent, for the kingdom of heaven has come near."
MATTHEW 4:17 NIV

What comes to mind when you hear the word *repent*? To repent means you truly regret your actions to the point where you turn in the opposite direction and walk the other way. You never go back to your sin. You couldn't bear to.

Lots of people feel sorry for what they've done. They feel guilty. But they don't truly repent. Jesus preached a full message—one that would change lives. He didn't say, "Make an apology and move on!" He said, "Repent, for the kingdom of heaven is near." To be more like Him, you'll need to do a few 180s!

I hear You loud and clear, Jesus. I'll do more than apologize
or ask for forgiveness. Give me the strength to turn away
from the things that are pulling me from You. Amen.

JESUS, FISHING FOR HEARTS

*Jesus called out to them, "Come, follow me,
and I will show you how to fish for people!"*
MATTHEW 4:19 NLT

Imagine fishing all night and catching nothing. Frustrating, right? All that effort. . .for nothing. If you've ever watched those survivor shows, you know how scary and dangerous it can be for the participants to cast their nets into the water, only to come up empty. No fish. No food.

Jesus wants us to fish for hearts. He longs for us to cast our nets toward a lost and broken world, to gently and lovingly draw in those who don't yet know Him.

If you're wondering how that's supposed to work, just follow His instructions in the verse above: "Come, follow me." When you set your eyes on Jesus, not the world, He will show you how to fish for people. . .the right way.

Jesus, my focus is on You! I trust that You will give me the courage and strategy to reach others so that they can fall in love with You. My net won't be empty when You're in charge. Amen.

JESUS, COMFORTING THOSE WHO MOURN

"God blesses those who mourn, for they will be comforted."
MATTHEW 5:4 NLT

God has promised to never leave us or forsake us. He's the great comforter, one who cares about what we're going through. No doubt you've experienced His gentle comfort in your life on multiple occasions.

That same compassion needs to live inside of each of His followers. He longs for us to comfort those who mourn. We have to take our eyes off of ourselves and notice what they're going through. Really notice. . .and care. Then we have to take the time to wrap the hurting in our arms and walk them through the valleys until sunlight comes again.

The comforted become the comforters. What a beautiful revelation.

---

*Thank You for comforting me, Jesus. Show me
how to be a comfort to others. Amen.*

JESUS, A MESSAGE OF PURITY

"God blesses those whose hearts are pure, for they will see God."
MATTHEW 5:8 NLT

In the twenty-first century, it's not always easy to maintain purity. Turn on the television, and you'll see shows with perverse language and sexual content. Stream a movie, and you might just get an earful or eyeful. Even the ads on TV are graphic at times.

It's no easier when you're out in public. The way people dress, the way they talk to each other. . .it's easy to see purity isn't front and center on their minds. And yet, Jesus wants you to strive for it if you long to be like Him.

Jesus spoke a message of purity but emphasized one key point: it starts with the heart. If you have clean hands and a pure heart, then the impurities of this world will stand in stark contrast. Keeping your heart pure will become a goal for the follower of Christ.

---

*I want to be pure like You, Jesus. Give me clean
hands and a pure heart, I pray. Amen.*

JESUS, A MESSAGE OF PEACE

"God blesses those who work for peace,
for they will be called the children of God."
Matthew 5:9 nlt

You know how it is. Your temper flares. You spout off. You lose your cool. Then, as soon as you get your emotions in check, you begin to regret your behavior. Oh, if only you could take back those harsh words that were spoken in anger. You would do it in a flash!

Jesus came with a message of peace. When you're His child, He desires for you to follow in His footsteps and keep that message of peace going. It's not always easy, but you really can be a peacemaker, even in the toughest of situations, if you keep your focus on Him.

I want to be a peacemaker, Jesus. Help me with my reactions,
I pray. I want to represent You well in all I do and say. Amen.

JESUS, COMPLETION OF THE LAW

"Do not think that I have come to do away with the Law of Moses or the writings of the early preachers. I have not come to do away with them but to complete them."

MATTHEW 5:17 NLV

What would happen if you wrote a sentence but never put a period at the end? It would go on and on forever. A period signifies completion. Your thought has ended as soon as you place that period. It doesn't nullify the sentence. On the contrary, it completes it.

Jesus was the period at the end of a spiritual sentence. God gave the Law in Old Testament times, but Jesus was the completion of that law. His coming signified the fulfillment of prophecies given by so many great men of God. He stopped the sentence in its tracks, shifting gears from one era to another—from the era of law to the era of grace.

He'll bring eras in your life to a stop too. Ask Him to become king of your heart, and He'll put a stop to your not-so-great yesterdays. He'll start a new sentence, a fresh one, filled with possibilities!

Thank You for fulfilling the Law, Jesus. Thank You for placing a period after my yesterdays and making all things new. Amen.

JESUS TEACHES US TO PRAY

"Pray like this: 'Our Father in heaven, Your name is holy. May Your holy nation come. What You want done, may it be done on earth as it is in heaven. Give us the bread we need today. Forgive us our sins as we forgive those who sin against us. Do not let us be tempted, but keep us from sin. Your nation is holy. You have power and shining-greatness forever. Let it be so.'"

MATTHEW 6:9–13 NLV

What is your prayer life like?

Perhaps some days it's better than others. On those frantic days, you might reach out to Jesus more frequently. Or maybe those are the days when it's harder to stay connected.

Jesus showed us how to pray when He spoke the words that we now call the Lord's Prayer. He led with a praise: "Your name is holy."

From there, He shifted to a heavenly perspective: "What You want done, may it be done on earth as it is in heaven." No doubt you need to have that same perspective over situations you're facing. Then He got down to business of daily needs. "Give us the bread we need today" was an afterthought to praise and acknowledgment of who God is.

Pray in heavenly order, and watch God move!

I praise You for who You are, Jesus.
Above all, I give You praise! Amen.

JESUS, OUR HEALER

*Jesus reached out and touched him. "I am willing," he said.
"Be healed!" And instantly the leprosy disappeared.*

MATTHEW 8:3 NLT

Jesus spent much of His ministry reaching out to those who were sick. He had compassion on them but didn't stop there. He actively participated in their healing. He reached out and touched the hurting ones and brought relief with His healing touch.

No doubt the Lord has healed you many times—either physically, emotionally, or spiritually. He cares about every facet of your life. And because you're created in His image, He wants you to speak healing over others. Take the time to pray for those who are sick. Visit them. Care for them. Take a meal or some cookies. Minister to those who are broken and hurting. Don't stop until healing comes.

Jesus, thank You for reminding me to pray for those who need healing—physically, psychologically, or otherwise. I'm so grateful You've healed so many areas of my life. I'll stand in the gap for those who are in need even now. Amen.

JESUS TEACHES US TO HAVE FAITH

Then Jesus said to the Roman officer, "Go back home. Because you believed, it has happened." And the young servant was healed that same hour.

MATTHEW 8:13 NLT

"Because you believed."

Wow! Those are powerful words that Jesus spoke over the Roman officer, aren't they? What if the man hadn't believed? Would Jesus still have healed him? It's interesting to think about, isn't it?

Jesus wants you to play an active role in the miracles He plans to perform in your life. He wants to increase your faith—not for His sake but your own. God could move without your participation, sure. But you would probably walk away and forget. When you participate in the miracle, it leaves a lasting memory.

Because you have believed. . .Jesus moves.

I get it, Jesus! Make my faith stronger. I want to believe for big things so that I can witness miracles. Amen.

JESUS, OWNER OF ALL

Jesus said to him, "Foxes have holes. Birds have nests.
But the Son of Man has no place to lay His head."

MATTHEW 8:20 NLV

It's ironic, isn't it? Jesus, who owns everything in the galaxy and beyond, was never a homeowner while here on earth. He never had a consistent place to lay His head. He had to depend on the kindness of others.

We put so much stock in what we own, don't we? We lay claim to houses, cars, clothes, and electronics. These things mean a lot to us. It's interesting to imagine what Jesus would say in response to all the items we supposedly own.

We can't take anything with us to heaven. They will soon become dust. So, pay more attention to your spiritual house. Give it to Jesus, the owner of the cattle on a thousand hills. Make Him the landlord of your heart.

Jesus, I own nothing! These things I care so much about are not eternal. They will drift away on the winds of time. Keep me focused on things that are eternal, the things that matter to You. Amen.

JESUS SPEAKS TO THE STORM

He said to them, "Why are you afraid? You have so little faith!" Then He stood up. He spoke sharp words to the wind and the waves. Then the wind stopped blowing.
MATTHEW 8:26 NLV

Jesus' words were more powerful than the storm that threatened to topple the boat He was on. Think about that for a moment. If you've ever been in a really awful storm, you know that it can be scary. High winds, rising floodwaters. . .the possibility for disaster is everywhere. And when your power is affected by the storm, you might find yourself facing that disaster in the dark.

Words of faith are stronger than the strongest storm. You can speak to the winds in your life. You can call out the name of Jesus over your situation and find the calm you need, even in the very center of the storm.

Increase your faith. Speak to the storm. You won't drown. Just keep your trust in Him.

I'll speak to the storms like You did, Jesus! Thank You for leading by example. I know I'll never drown because You're in the boat with me. Amen.

JESUS, MOVED BY OUR FAITH

*They took a man to Him who was on his bed. This man
was not able to move his body. Jesus saw their faith.
He said, "Son, take hope. Your sins are forgiven."*
MATTHEW 9:2 NLV

Have you ever been moved by someone else's pain? Maybe you
witnessed an accident and actually felt the pain the victim was going
through. Or perhaps you walked a friend through a divorce and
felt her pain as she severed the relationship with her once husband.

We are easily moved by pain, but Jesus was easily moved by
faith. When He saw the faith of the people, He was spurred to
action. The same is true today. When you're going through a rough
patch and your faith is low, you can still activate your faith. When
you do, it sets the wheels in motion for God to move. He's moved
by your faith. Today, give Him something to work with. Activate
that faith and watch Him move!

---

*Lord, thank You for being moved by my trust in You.
I can't wait to see what You're going to do in my
life now that my faith is activated. Amen.*

JESUS KNOWS WHAT WE'RE THINKING

Jesus knew what they were thinking. He said, "Why do you think bad thoughts in your hearts? Which is easier to say, 'Your sins are forgiven,' or to say, 'Get up and walk?' But this is to show you that the Son of Man has power on earth to forgive sins." He said to the sick man, "Get up! Take your bed and go home."

MATTHEW 9:4–6 NLV

Have you ever been relieved that the people in the room couldn't see the thoughts tumbling around in your head? Sometimes our thoughts are a bit off-putting. But here's the thing: Jesus sees it all. The frustration. The anger. The joy. The things you want to say. He's a witness to the thoughts, even when no one else can see or hear.

And, in spite of that, He loves you. He's not standing there, finger waggling. He's gently wooing you back to Himself, saying, "Come on now, girl. You know better than that."

It's not always easy to control your thoughts, but the Bible does say that we can be transformed by the renewing of our minds. If we give our thoughts to Him, we become more like Him in all we do, say, and yes. . .even think.

Thank You for taking control of my thoughts, Jesus. Amen.

JESUS IS LOOKING FOR FOLLOWERS

As Jesus went from there, He saw a man called Matthew. Matthew was sitting at his work gathering taxes. Jesus said to him, "Follow Me." Matthew got up and followed Jesus.
MATTHEW 9:9 NLV

Imagine you're at work, doing your thing, when a stranger approaches and says, "Follow me." You would probably look at him and say, "Um, excuse me?" Chances are close to zero that you would actually leave everything you know to follow a stranger.

In the case of the disciples, following Jesus turned out to be the best decision they could have made. And, if you've given your heart to Him, the decision to follow Him was the best decision you've ever made too.

Following someone means you trust that they know where they're going. Jesus sees into the future, so you can most assuredly trust Him with your tomorrows.

I'll follow hard after You, Jesus! I'm so glad You can see the road ahead. I trust You to lead me every step of the way. Amen.

JESUS, FRIEND TO SINNERS

On hearing this, Jesus said, "It is not the healthy who need a doctor, but the sick. But go and learn what this means: 'I desire mercy, not sacrifice.' For I have not come to call the righteous, but sinners."

MATTHEW 9:12–13 NIV

Jesus led by example when He befriended sinners. His love for mankind extended to all, no matter the lifestyle choices.

Sometimes, it's hard to know how to find a balance when it comes to friendship choices, right? You want to befriend sinners, but you don't want to get caught up in their questionable lifestyles or drama. You don't want to change your belief system because they expect you to.

Here's the thing: Jesus never left people in their sinful state. He entered those relationships with the solid understanding that following Him—entering into relationship with Him—would result in a changed life.

Be like Jesus. Include others while keeping your expectations high. Lives can be changed. There can be turnaround. Stand in the gap, and watch God move.

You are a life-changer, Jesus. I trust You to move in the hearts of those I love. Amen.

JESUS OFFERS HOPE

Jesus turned and saw her. "Take heart, daughter,"
he said, "your faith has healed you." And the
woman was healed at that moment.
MATTHEW 9:22 NIV

Have you ever been in a situation where hopelessness creeped in? It's hard to snap out of that mind-set once it hits, isn't it?

Jesus never leaves us hopeless. In fact, hope is such a priceless commodity that He wants to infuse us with it, no matter what circumstances we're facing. In the hospital undergoing chemotherapy? Speak life over your situation. Dealing with a child who's running from the Lord? Keep your hope alive by praying scriptures over him. Facing a difficult situation at work or school? Think about how Jesus would handle that situation, then lift your chin and move forward, knowing He has an answer for any problem you might be facing.

Knowing He has answers always infuses hope, so keep your eyes on Him not the problem.

I'm so grateful You're the giver of hope, Jesus. I will
keep my eyes on You, no matter how difficult the
circumstances. Infuse me with hope, I pray. Amen.

JESUS IS LOOKING FOR WORKERS

Then he said to his disciples, "The harvest is plentiful
but the workers are few. Ask the Lord of the harvest,
therefore, to send out workers into his harvest field."

MATTHEW 9:37–38 NIV

There's work to be done, and Jesus hopes you'll step up to the plate and help carry the load. This world is filled with people who need to know Him, and they'll only hear the gospel message if folks like you are courageous and speak up.

It's not easy, especially these days. Christianity flies in the face of current social norms. But the gospel hasn't changed and never will. Best of all, it has the power to transform hearts and lives.

Today, be like Isaiah (in the sixth chapter). He stood in the temple and proclaimed, "Here am I, Lord. Send me." Offer yourself in service to God, and you will never be sorry about the outcome. He will use you in ways you never dreamed possible.

I want to be used by You, Jesus. Here am I. . .send me! I don't
know what that looks like, but I trust You to use me in a way
that works with my personality and my spiritual gifts. Amen.

JESUS CALLS US TO TAKE UP OUR CROSS

*"Whoever does not take up their cross and
follow me is not worthy of me."*
MATTHEW 10:38 NIV

What do you suppose Jesus meant when He said that we should "take up our cross" and follow Him? What cross, specifically?

Following after the Lord isn't always easy. There are costs to being a person of faith. You'll be ridiculed at times and ostracized for differences in belief. Those who are worldlier might lash out at you if you refuse to bend to their belief systems.

You'll have to take up your cross many times over in this life, but Jesus made it clear that our willingness to carry our cross is essential. We prove our worthiness by our willingness.

As a believer, what cross has been hardest for you to carry? Instead of fighting it, ask for His strength to carry it all the way.

*I'll do my best to carry my cross, Jesus. I know that
my burdens are eased when I place them in Your
hands, so that's what I choose to do today. Amen.*

JESUS, YOUR WAY TO THE FATHER

"All things have been committed to me by my Father. No one knows the Son except the Father, and no one knows the Father except the Son and those to whom the Son chooses to reveal him."

MATTHEW 11:27 NIV

Remember those mazes you used to work as a child? You would place your pencil down at the START mark and follow the various paths until you ran into a dead end. Then you would begin again, taking a different path until you finally found the one that led you out.

In the Amish country, you can visit cornfield mazes that are similar. It's easy to get lost inside!

Life is kind of like that maze. You'll run into a lot of dead ends until you finally give your heart to Jesus. He's the only way to the Father, so you'll want to stick with Him from start to finish.

Going your own way? It might seem fine at first, but you'll hit a wall every time.

I'm tired of dead ends, Jesus. I'll stick with You! Amen.

JESUS, GREATER THAN THE LAW

Jesus answered, "What if one of you has a sheep and it falls into a deep hole on the Sabbath? Will you not take hold of it and lift it out? And a human being is worth much more than a sheep! So then, our Law does allow us to help someone on the Sabbath."

MATTHEW 12:11–12 GNT

The Pharisees and Sadducees were always trying to set Jesus up. They thought if they could catch Him breaking Levitical law, they would prove He was a fraud. But Jesus was always one step ahead of them. He knew what they did not—that He was greater than the Law.

This beautiful story about the sheep falling into a hole on the Sabbath was the perfect way to catch them at their own game. He came to rescue humanity, after all, and humans are worth much more than sheep. He chose (and continues to choose) to heal, save, and deliver us, no matter the day or the hour. Even on the Sabbath.

Jesus broke with tradition to tend to the lost. Imagine that.

I get it, Jesus! You weren't as worried about traditions as You were about souls. Thank You for the reminder that it's the people who matter most to You. Amen.

JESUS EXPLAINS OUR FAMILY

Jesus answered, "Who is my mother? Who are my brothers?"
Then he pointed to his disciples and said, "Look! Here are
my mother and my brothers! Whoever does what my Father
in heaven wants is my brother, my sister, and my mother."
MATTHEW 12:48–50 GNT

Family is everything. No doubt you would fight tooth and nail to protect yours. But Jesus came with a message that seemed to fly in the face of what we think of as family. He broadened the net when He explained that our family is actually much larger than we think.

All who call on the name of Jesus are linked in the family tree. That woman at church who grates on your nerves. That neighbor who mows his lawn at seven in the morning. That coworker who often messes things up. All who claim Christ as Lord and Savior are brothers and sisters. As with any family, there will be quarrels. But remember, Jesus came to bind us together in love, so open your heart to a bigger, wider table.

Thank You for including all of us in Your family,
Lord. I'm happy to sit at the table. Amen.

JESUS SHARES PARABLES

Jesus told them another parable: "The Kingdom of heaven is like this. A man takes a mustard seed and sows it in his field. It is the smallest of all seeds, but when it grows up, it is the biggest of all plants. It becomes a tree, so that birds come and make their nests in its branches."

MATTHEW 13:31–32 GNT

When you think of a mustard seed, no doubt you imagine that teensy-tiny seed encased in glass, hanging on a necklace, a lovely little reminder of your faith.

What if you pictured yourself planting that tiny seed in the ground? You dig (going deep with God in worship and prayer), then you drop in the seed and cover it with dirt.

What happens next?

You step back...and wait. The seed has disappeared from sight. It's up to God now. But you know He's trustworthy. He's never let you down in the past, and He won't this time either.

He'll take your tiny seed and grow it into something magnificent, sweet woman of God. Just wait and see.

I trust You in the waiting, Jesus. Amen.

JESUS TEACHES US NOT TO FEAR

Jesus spoke to them at once. "Courage!"
he said. "It is I. Don't be afraid!"
MATTHEW 14:27 GNT

Have you ever been completely knotted up in fear? Maybe you found yourself trapped in your home during a tornado or hurricane. Winds howled outside of your door. You wondered if the roof would hold.

Or perhaps you found yourself at the bedside of a dying loved one, tears streaming down your face.

Even in the deepest, darkest valley, Jesus tells us not to fear. He doesn't add, "This will be easy." He knows it will be hard. But you really can look fear directly in the face and speak to it, in Jesus' name. It has to flee at the mention of His powerful name.

No matter how big. No matter how dark. No matter how scary. Fear must go.

Thank You for giving me the courage to drive away fear,
Lord! I speak to it today, in Jesus' name! Amen.

JESUS PROVIDES WHAT WE NEED

*Then he took the seven loaves and the fish, gave thanks
to God, broke them, and gave them to the disciples; and
the disciples gave them to the people. They all ate and
had enough. Then the disciples took up seven baskets
full of pieces left over. The number of men who ate was
four thousand, not counting the women and children.*

MATTHEW 15:36–38 GNT

Have you ever experienced an eleventh-hour miracle? There you
are, at the height of "This is never going to work out!" and Jesus
comes through for you. He provides what you need just when
you need it.

That's what happened in this popular Bible story. Thousands
of people had gathered to hear Jesus speak, and they were hungry.
This miracle wasn't planned out in advance. Right then, right
there. . .in the moment. . .Jesus stepped in and provided what the
people needed.

The Bible doesn't promise He'll give you want you want, only
what you need.

What do you need today? Don't fret. It's coming.

Thank You, my provider, for giving me all I need and more! Amen.

JESUS IS THE CHRIST, THE SON OF GOD

He said to them, "But who do you say that I am?" Simon Peter said, "You are the Christ, the Son of the living God."

MATTHEW 16:15–16 NLV

Who do you say that Jesus is? If someone asked, "What's your take on Jesus? Who is He, anyway?" what would you say?

Peter responded with the ultimate all-in-one answer: "You are the Christ, the Son of the living God." In those few words, he acknowledged the divinity of Jesus as well as His lordship in Peter's life. He also called God "living," acknowledging the Lord's active participation in his life.

Who do you say that Jesus is? Today, if you don't know the answer to that question, it's time to ask for a fresh revelation—of who He is and who He wants to be in your life.

Lord, today I come to you afresh, asking You to be both Lord and Savior. I acknowledge You as King of the universe, Creator of all. I ask You to come and live in my heart and to take the reins of my life. May I say with Peter, "You are the Christ, the Son of the living God!"

JESUS WAS A STRAIGHT SHOOTER

Then Jesus turned to Peter and said, "Get behind Me,
Satan! You are standing in My way. You are not thinking
how God thinks. You are thinking how man thinks."

MATTHEW 16:23 NLV

Jesus didn't mince words. He said what He meant, and He meant what He said—even if His words sounded shocking to those around Him.

What about you? Are you a straight shooter, or do you stumble-bumble over your words? It's not always easy to speak hard truth, is it? And to speak it in love? Even harder!

Still, if you want to be like Jesus, you need to try. Speak His truth with as much love as you can muster. Speak it when you stand in the face of opposition. Speak it when your heart feels weak. Speak it when the world shouts an opposite message.

And remember the point of Jesus' message to Peter: "You're not thinking like I think!" To be more like Him, you have to have His perspective on absolutely everything!

I want to think like You, speak like You, and have Your perspective,
Jesus. Today, I give You my will, my thoughts, and my mouth.
Have Your way in all those areas of my life, I pray. Amen.

JESUS TEACHES US TO MOVE MOUNTAINS

Jesus said to them, "Because you have so little faith. For sure, I tell you, if you have faith as a mustard seed, you will say to this mountain, 'Move from here to over there,' and it would move over. You will be able to do anything. But this kind of demon does not go out but by prayer and by going without food so you can pray better."
MATTHEW 17:20–21 NLV

No doubt you've faced a lot of mountains in your life. Some of them loom large. You think you'll never get past them. A cancer diagnosis. An unwanted divorce. The loss of a child. You stare at the mountain in shock and disbelief, convinced it will never move and that you will live in its shadow forever.

Jesus gave such an amazing illustration when He told us to speak to the mountains in our lives. He knows (of course) that we're most intimidated when facing something huge. But if we can summon the courage to increase our faith and speak vocally to the very thing that's overwhelming us, we stand a much better chance of watching it fall!

Speak to your mountain today. Let the words propel your faith.

Jesus, thank You for giving me the courage to speak to the mountains in my life! Amen.

JESUS PREDICTED HIS DEATH AND RESURRECTION

While they were still in Galilee, Jesus said to the followers, "The Son of Man will be handed over to men. They will kill Him, but He will be raised from the dead three days later." The followers were very sad.

MATTHEW 17:22–23 NLV

You wouldn't be human if you hadn't pondered your own death. Maybe you won't know how you'll go. . .and when. It's probably for the best that you don't know the answers to those questions, or they would become the focus of your remaining years.

Jesus knew the time, the date, and the details of His impending death. He knew, and yet He didn't allow the fear of death to change anything about how He lived. He went on healing, went on loving, went on teaching and sharing the message of hope to the masses.

Jesus knew the ultimate secret: He would rise from the dead on the third day. Death pales in the face of resurrection power! Like Jesus, believers will be resurrected, raised to live forever in heaven. Once you give your heart to Him, eternity is yours for the taking!

Thank You for the promise of eternal life, Jesus! Amen.

JESUS WANTS US TO COME AS CHILDREN

"So anyone who becomes as humble as this little child is the greatest in the Kingdom of Heaven. And anyone who welcomes a little child like this on my behalf is welcoming me."

MATTHEW 18:4–5 NLT

Have you ever had a conversation with a young child? Most are so innocent, so wide-eyed and filled with wonder, that they will amuse and delight you with their comments. They face life with an enthusiasm that seems to fade with age.

What if it didn't fade? What if you faced all that life offers—good and bad—through the eyes of a child? What if your faith was as strong as it was when you were two, when you trusted your parents absolutely—to feed, clothe, and care for you.

Jesus wants you to come as a child. Even on the bad days. Even when you're facing a season of lack. Come with wide-eyed wonder, filled with trust in your heavenly Father, the one who has always taken care of you.

---

*I come today with the faith and humility of a child, Lord.
I trust You completely. You're my good, good Father! Amen.*

JESUS, IN OUR MIDST

*"For where two or three gather together as my
followers, I am there among them."*
MATTHEW 18:20 NLT

Jesus is with you right now. It might be hard to wrap your head around this concept, but it's 100 percent true. He's not only in the room, He's in your heart. He knows your thoughts. He understands your motives.

He's there, and He sees what you're going through. He empathizes with your pain. He cares about the things you care about.

Now think about that principle when it comes to gathering with fellow believers. There's power in numbers. When two or three (or ten or twenty) come together to petition God for something, He's right there, in the midst of them.

Hang out with fellow believers, and you will be a force to be reckoned with!

---

*Thank You for always being in our midst, Jesus. You
will never leave us or forsake us! May Your church
be a force for good in this world! Amen.*

JESUS GIVES A LESSON ON FORGIVENESS

Then Peter came to him and asked, "Lord, how often should I forgive someone who sins against me? Seven times?" "No, not seven times," Jesus replied, "but seventy times seven!"

<small>MATTHEW 18:21–22 NLT</small>

"I don't feel like forgiving her. She doesn't deserve it." How many times have you voiced those words? (Okay, so maybe you haven't said them aloud, but you've probably had that thought flit through your mind at some point!)

People don't deserve forgiveness. That's true. Many times, they mess up and never acknowledge what they've done. They don't attempt to clean up the mess they've caused. But even then, Jesus calls us to forgive anyway.

He forgave you, didn't He? Think of all those things—the embarrassing things, the shameful things, the impulsive things—you did. And He goes on forgiving today, tomorrow, and until you're in heaven with Him.

If you want to be like Jesus, you must forgive. Deep breath, girl. You can do this.

Okay, I get it, Jesus. I'll forgive those who have hurt me, even the ones I (truly) don't want to forgive. Show me how to let go, I pray. Amen.

JESUS' PLAN FOR SUCCESS

Jesus told him, "If you want to be perfect, go and sell all your possessions and give the money to the poor, and you will have treasure in heaven. Then come, follow me."
MATTHEW 19:21 NLT

God's plans don't always make sense, do they? He told a blind man to wash his eyes in the pool of Siloam. He told a man whose child had died that the little one was merely sleeping. And He told us—all of us—that if we want to be successful, we must be willing to give up (literally) everything. These are head scratchers, for sure!

Picture yourself in the shoes of the rich young ruler. Jesus has just said, "If you really want to be perfect, sell all your stuff and come follow Me." How would you react?

Most would turn and walk the other way! But if you dig a bit deeper, you see that Jesus is just trying to go deep with us. He wants our hearts. And if they're wound around the things of this world, they won't be available to Him.

Unwind your heart. Give it to Him afresh today.

I won't get caught up in worldly possessions, Jesus. My heart is Yours! Amen.

JESUS GIVES PERSPECTIVE ON POSSESSIONS

Jesus said to His followers, "For sure, I tell you, it will be hard for a rich man to get into the holy nation of heaven."
MATTHEW 19:23 NLV

It's kind of ironic, isn't it? Heaven has gates of pearl and streets of gold—the very things a rich person would love. Yet, Jesus says it's hard for a rich man to get into heaven to enjoy those things.

Here's the point: when you've fallen in love with the possessions of this life, your focus is on them, not Him. Jesus wants your full attention. If you're easily distracted by bright and shiny objects—if you give your heart to every passing fancy—then it's going to be impossible to put Him first.

Having the right perspective will shape your life and your relationship with Jesus. And don't worry about earthly possessions! One day, you'll spend eternity with the one who owns the cattle on a thousand hills! He has amazing things waiting for you in heaven.

I won't be distracted by bright and shiny objects, Jesus. I'll keep my eyes on You. Someday soon, I'll walk on streets of gold! Amen.

JESUS PREACHES HOLY ORDER

"Many who are first will be last.
Many who are last will be first."
MATTHEW 19:30 NLV

Do you like to follow Hollywood stars? Maybe you're fascinated with their romances or the homes they live in. Perhaps you're intrigued by their clothing choices or their hyped-up awards ceremonies. When it comes to twenty-first-century humans, "superstars" certainly get a lot of attention.

Don't you love Jesus' perspective on such things? He makes one thing very clear to His followers: the first will be last and the last will be first.

The woman who can't pay her light bill. The man who's battling cancer. The child who's struggling in poverty. The godly young woman who pours herself out to help her friends in need.

Jesus wants you to see past the superstars to the true "firsts" in this world. They're right in front of you, day in and day out.

Can you see them?

I see them, Jesus! And I won't look past them to the ones whose stars seem to be shining brighter. Help me to represent You well. . .with the first and the last and all in between. Amen.

JESUS SEES THE PAIN THAT IS COMING

"Listen! We are going up to Jerusalem. The Son of Man will be handed over to the religious leaders and to the teachers of the Law. They will say that He must be put to death. They will hand Him over to the people who do not know God. They will make fun of Him and will beat Him. They will nail Him to a cross. Three days later He will be raised to life."
MATTHEW 20:18–19 NLV

Jesus knew that He would be put to death. He knew that He would experience agonizing pain, even ahead of that, at the hands of the Roman soldiers.

He knew it all, and yet He still chose to go through with it. He could have skipped that whole trip back to Jerusalem and said to His Father, "I've had a change of heart, sorry." But He didn't. In spite of knowing the pain ahead, He walked the road anyway.

He sees into your tomorrows too. He sees the good days and the tough ones. But He's prepared to walk that road with you, no matter what it brings.

You can trust Him in the journey, friend. Even the painful journey.

You know, Jesus. I put my hand in Yours as I walk this path, knowing that You can see clearly into tomorrow and won't ever leave my side. Amen.

JESUS CARES MORE ABOUT OTHERS THAN HIMSELF

For the Son of Man came not to be cared for. He came to care for others. He came to give His life so that many could be bought by His blood and made free from the punishment of sin.
MATTHEW 20:28 NLV

When it came to putting others first, Jesus led the way. In the middle of a good night's sleep? No problem. His disciples needed Him to calm a storm. . .He calmed a storm. Tired after preaching for hours on end? No worries. Thousands of people needed food, and He was there to make sure they got it.

Jesus went above and beyond, always thinking of others first. This servant-oriented heart led Him all the way to the cross.

If you want to be like Jesus, turn your focus from yourself to those around you. It's not always easy. It's human nature to think of yourself first. But having an others-focused mentality will enrich your life and change its trajectory.

Turn my vision outward I pray, Jesus! Amen.

JESUS, THE GREATEST ONE!

*The people who went in front and those who followed
Jesus called out, "Greatest One! The Son of David!
Great and honored is He Who comes in the name of
the Lord! Greatest One in the highest heaven."*

MATTHEW 21:9 NLV

Who's the greatest person you know? Someone you greatly admire.
A teacher? A friend? Someone you work with? A pastor or church
leader? Likely, someone sprang to mind when you read that question.

It's great to admire people, especially those who are doing
wonderful things with their lives or impressive things for the
kingdom of God. And it's also wonderful when people admire us
because they see Christ in us and in our actions.

That said, there is one who is to be admired above all others.
Jesus is the greatest of all. He outranks everyone else! So, next time
you want to call on someone with clout, turn to Him. You won't
be disappointed!

---

*u rank the highest, Jesus! There is none higher.
turn to You, maker of all and author of all! Amen.*

JESUS GIVES
PERSPECTIVE ON FAITH

*Jesus said to them, "For sure, I tell you this: If you have
faith and do not doubt, you will not only be able to do
what was done to the fig tree. You will also be able to
say to this mountain, 'Move from here and be thrown
into the sea,' and it will be done. All things you ask
for in prayer, you will receive if you have faith."*
MATTHEW 21:21–22 NLV

If someone said, "Check your perspective, girl," how would you
take it? What are they really trying to say to you?

Jesus offers perspective in the verse above. "If you have faith
and do not doubt. . ." Those are powerful words. And they give a
front-end perspective to the rest of the principle, "then you can
move mountains."

God could move them without you, of course, but He wants you
to have a faith-filled perspective, one that looks at mountains with
joy in your heart, knowing they're about to be tossed into the sea.

Do you have that perspective today?

---

*I want to have that kind of faith, Jesus. Give me Your
perspective when I face mountains! Amen.*

JESUS LINES UP THE LAWS

Jesus said to him, " 'You must love the Lord your God with all your heart and with all your soul and with all your mind.' This is the first and greatest of the Laws. The second is like it, 'You must love your neighbor as you love yourself.' All the Laws and the writings of the early preachers depend on these two most important Laws."

MATTHEW 22:37–40 NLV

There were a lot of laws to follow in Old Testament times. Hundreds of them. Maybe thousands! It was probably really overwhelming for the people to keep up with all of it.

Then Jesus came along and, in His succinct way, summed it all up in just a few words: "Love God; love people."

What a difference we would make in this world if we all truly strived to live like that. If we loved God above all (above ourselves, our wishes, our wants, our dreams) and loved people as much as we love ourselves. (Harder than it looks!)

Love is the answer. And when we fall in love with Him, He teaches us how to love others. . .even the unlovable ones.

Show me how to love, Jesus. I know that love is the greatest law of all, and it's one You've written on my heart. Amen.

THE WORDS OF JESUS STAND FOREVER!

"Heaven and earth will pass away,
but my words will never pass away."
Matthew 24:35 niv

Have you ever tried to remember a conversation you had in the past? Even recent conversations are difficult to remember. Our words come out at rapid-fire pace, and we don't often think them through before speaking. No wonder we can't bring them to mind later on!

The words of Jesus are completely different. Aren't you glad we have the Bible (the written Word) so that we never forget what He told us? His words are solid gold to us. They're life-giving. And they're just as powerful now as they were when He first spoke them.

Heaven and earth will pass away, but the things Jesus told us? His instructions for living and His plan of salvation for humankind? Those will last through all eternity!

You are a God of Your word! I can trust what You've told me, Jesus! Those life-giving words last forever! Amen.

JESUS COMMENDS THE UNLOVELY

Aware of this, Jesus said to them, "Why are you bothering this woman? She has done a beautiful thing to me. The poor you will always have with you, but you will not always have me. When she poured this perfume on my body, she did it to prepare me for burial. Truly I tell you, wherever this gospel is preached throughout the world, what she has done will also be told, in memory of her."

MATTHEW 26:10–13 NIV

Jesus dealt with a lot of "unlovely" people during His lifetime. He dined with sinners, healed the broken, even came in close contact with prostitutes, thieves, lepers, and other untouchables. And He loved them all the same.

No matter how unlovely you might feel at times, no matter what sort of sins you've committed in your past, Jesus loves you as much as the finest person out there. And let's be honest: the "finest" are all sinners too. The truth is, we're all "unlovely," but to Him, we're all beautiful.

Thank You for seeing us as lovely, Jesus! While I see my sins, my flaws, You see a child of the Most High King! I'm grateful for Your holy vision! Amen.

JESUS SPEAKS OF HIS BODY AND BLOOD

While they were eating, Jesus took bread, and when he had given thanks, he broke it and gave it to his disciples, saying, "Take and eat; this is my body." Then he took a cup, and when he had given thanks, he gave it to them, saying, "Drink from it, all of you. This is my blood of the covenant, which is poured out for many for the forgiveness of sins. I tell you, I will not drink from this fruit of the vine from now on until that day when I drink it new with you in my Father's kingdom."

MATTHEW 26:26–29 NIV

Don't you love the covenant (agreement) Jesus made with us? Through the shedding of His own blood and the breaking of His own body, He bought our salvation.

Jesus recognized the power of His body and blood and spoke of this when He shared communion with His disciples that final night before His crucifixion.

And now, two thousand–plus years later, that blood is just as powerful as it was back then. When we take the bread, we're reminded that His body was broken just for us. What a gift from our Savior. He truly gave us His all!

Thank You for the blood that cleanses me from sin, Jesus! Thank You for Your body, broken and bruised for me! What a sacrifice. What a Savior! I'm forever grateful. Amen.

JESUS ASKS FOR THE CUP TO BE REMOVED FROM HIM

*Going a little farther, he fell with his face to the ground
and prayed, "My Father, if it is possible, may this cup
be taken from me. Yet not as I will, but as you will."*

MATTHEW 26:39 NIV

Have you ever wished you could back out of something even before it happened? Maybe you were invited to a party but didn't care to go. You said yes, then regretted it. Or maybe you agreed to do a certain task but reached the eleventh hour with huge regrets.

It's not always easy to follow through, is it?

It should bring you great comfort to know that even Jesus had questions. He prayed, "God, if it's possible, remove this from Me. Still, Your will, not Mine."

What a model prayer! Maybe it's time we approach God with the same attitude: "Lord, I don't really want to do this, but I do want to please Your heart. If You choose not to take this from me, then give me the courage to move forward. Not my will, but Yours be done."

---

*I pray those words today, Lord! Not my will, but
Yours! Even if it's hard. Even if I feel like I can't.
I want to please Your heart, Father. Amen.*

JESUS REMINDS US WHO'S IN CHARGE

"Don't you know that I could call on my Father for help, and at once he would send me more than twelve armies of angels?"

MATTHEW 26:53 GNT

Jesus had a way of letting His disciples know who was in charge! He's not just the King of the universe, He's got an army of angels on His side. And guess what? They're on your side too!

When your enemy rears his ugly head, remind him whose team you're on. And, more importantly, who's on your team. You have the Father, Son, and Holy Spirit. And you have multiple armies of angels.

On top of all that, you've been given gifts of the Spirit. You're fully equipped, girl. You might not always feel like it, but as a daughter of the King, you're a force to be reckoned with!

Lord, I don't always feel powerful. Sometimes, I feel small and insignificant. But You're with me. And You've given me all I need to get through the challenges I face. I'm grateful for that army of angels! Amen.

JESUS, RIDICULED BY HIS ENEMIES

*Above his head they put the written notice of the accusation
against him: "This is Jesus, the King of the Jews."*
MATTHEW 27:37 GNT

Being ridiculed is never any fun—whether those ridiculing are
intentionally trying to hurt you or otherwise.

You have a Savior who understands and empathizes. He was
beaten, mocked, and hung to die in front of His accusers. He fully
gets it when you're feeling hurt by others. He's been hurt too. When
you've been mocked? He says, "Girl, I was mocked too. And I let
those words roll right off of Me."

We know He did because He somehow kept going in the face
of the ridicule. He turned the other cheek and gave His all—for
them and for you.

---

*Jesus, You've been through it all. There's nothing I can
ever face that You haven't already faced. You've been
mocked and ridiculed. You were wounded by those who
claimed to love You. You understand and You care about
all I've been through. How grateful I am. Amen.*

JESUS FELT ABANDONED

At about three o'clock Jesus cried out with a loud shout, "Eli, Eli, lema sabachthani?" which means, "My God, my God, why did you abandon me?"
MATTHEW 27:46 GNT

No doubt you've suffered feelings of abandonment. You've felt alone. Lost. Scared. You wondered if anyone else even noticed what you were going through.

Jesus sees. Jesus cares. Jesus has walked a mile in your shoes. He suffered the ultimate feelings of abandonment in those hours that He hung on the cross. And when He cried out, "My God, My God, why have You forsaken Me?," He truly felt forsaken. Lost. Unseen.

The next time you're struggling with "Do they see me?," remember this scene on the cross. When no one else sees or seems to care. . .He does.

I'm so grateful You see into my loneliness, Jesus. I'm so sorry for all You went through, but I'm so touched to know that You get it. You understand. Amen.

JESUS WAS LABELED A LIAR

*The next day, which was a Sabbath, the chief priests
and the Pharisees met with Pilate and said, "Sir,
we remember that while that liar was still alive he
said, 'I will be raised to life three days later.' "*

MATTHEW 27:62–63 GNT

Have you ever been falsely accused? Maybe someone said you
did something that you didn't really do. There's no worse feeling
than knowing you're innocent but you're unable to prove it. Talk
about feeling stuck!

Jesus feels your pain. Though He never committed a sin in His
life, though He never once told a lie (How could He?), Jesus was
falsely accused of being a liar. When He claimed to be the Son of
God (a big claim, clearly), only His followers believed Him. The
religious leaders were convinced He was nothing but a fraud. And
when He said He would rise from the dead? Well, even some of
His followers were probably doubtful.

When you feel like no one gets it, Jesus does.

---

*I'm so sorry You were falsely accused, Lord. How that must have
broken Your heart. Help me to remember, when I'm up against
a false accusation, that You overcame and I can too. Amen.*

JESUS LEFT THE TOMB

The angel spoke to the women. "You must not be afraid,"
he said. "I know you are looking for Jesus, who was
crucified. He is not here; he has been raised, just as he
said. Come here and see the place where he was lying."

MATTHEW 28:5–6 GNT

Even death couldn't take Jesus down. Think about that for a moment. Have you ever known anyone else who died and came back to life? Sure, there are a few stories here and there of people who died for a few minutes, then miraculously survived.

But to die, be buried, and rise again on the third day? No one in the history of the world has ever done that. . .except Jesus.

He tasted death and lived to tell about it. He left His graveclothes behind and walked out of that tomb.

No matter what you're going through today—no matter what graveclothes you're wearing—you can be like your Savior. He can resurrect you from the tombs that have you bound. He can restore you to new life again.

You can restore me even when I'm wrapped in graveclothes,
Jesus! Thank You for resurrection power! Amen.

JESUS HAS BEEN GIVEN ALL AUTHORITY

Jesus drew near and said to them, "I have been given all authority in heaven and on earth."
MATTHEW 28:18 GNT

Have you ever met someone who had a problem with authority? Maybe a child you know likes to sass her parents. Or maybe a coworker has trouble submitting to what the boss needs her to do. Perhaps that teenage boy you know struggles with his authority figures at school.

It happens.

Jesus is the ultimate authority. And when He told His followers that all authority had been given to Him, not just here on earth but in heaven too? They had to see right then and there that He really was who He said He was.

You can speak the name of Jesus, and it carries that same weight, that same authority. What problem are you going through today? Speak the name of the one whose name is above every name!

I come to You, the ultimate authority, Jesus! I speak Your name, knowing You have the power to move heaven and earth! Take charge of my situation, I pray. Amen.

JESUS COMMISSIONS US

"Go, then, to all peoples everywhere and make them my disciples: baptize them in the name of the Father, the Son, and the Holy Spirit, and teach them to obey everything I have commanded you. And I will be with you always, to the end of the age."

MATTHEW 28:19–20 GNT

If you've ever served in the military, you know what it's like to be commissioned to do a job. You're given marching orders; and your role, should you choose to accept it, is to follow those orders. There's no deviating from those in authority.

Before Jesus ascended into heaven, He gave His disciples a great commission. He asked them to go into all the world (no small task) and make disciples.

This must have felt impossible to them at the time, but they didn't hesitate. Those disciples hit the road and spread the gospel all across Asia and beyond. If they hadn't had the courage to go, you might never know today. We owe them so much!

Today, it's actually possible to go into the whole world. We have the internet and modern technology. If the disciples could do it, we should do it too!

I'll do my part, Jesus. I'll share the gospel message to people I meet along the way. Amen.

JESUS IS PROPELLED BY OUR FAITH

Seeing how much faith they had, Jesus said to the paralyzed man, "My son, your sins are forgiven."
MARK 2:5 GNT

In the verse above, Jesus was activated by the faith of a few people. Their faith propelled Him to action. He healed the paralyzed man as a direct result of the faith of the man's friends.

Do you have the kind of faith to propel God to action? That's a tough thing to think about, isn't it? Maybe your faith is only mustard seed-size at this very moment. That's okay. Jesus said a teensy-tiny amount was enough to move mountains.

Today, do what you can to grow your faith. Activate it, and watch God move on your behalf. And remember, if Jesus was moved to action because of the faith of a man's friends, you can be that friend to others. Pray for those in need. Pray for those who lack faith. Pray for the hurting. Perhaps your faith will activate a holy God to action!

I come to You today, Lord, filled with faith—for my own needs and the needs of those I love! Amen.

JESUS CLARIFIES HIS CALL

Jesus heard them and answered, "People who are well do not need a doctor, but only those who are sick. I have not come to call respectable people, but outcasts."

MARK 2:17 GNT

Jesus came for the outcasts. That should bring you great comfort if you've ever felt pushed to the edge of the crowd. He came for the ones who didn't fit in. The excluded. The different. The weak. The unsure.

When you feel like you're outside of societal norms (you're not in the clique), don't fret. Jesus didn't fit in either. But He came to preach the gospel to all mankind, not just those who fit a certain demographic.

You weren't made to fit in. You were made to stand out. So, go on shining for Him, and don't worry about where you fit in the grand scheme of things. All that matters is that Jesus came for you too.

I don't always feel like part of the crowd, Jesus. I know You know what that feels like. Thank You for coming for the outcasts. Amen.

JESUS WALKS ON WATER

But they saw him walking on the water. "It's a ghost!"
they thought, and screamed. They were all terrified
when they saw him. Jesus spoke to them at once,
"Courage!" he said. "It is I. Don't be afraid!"

MARK 6:49–50 GNT

Picture this: The disciples are on board a boat when they see a figure out on the water, walking toward them. They panic. (No doubt you would too.) Thinking they're seeing a ghost, they let out a scream. Or two. Or three.

From where He stands atop the waves, Jesus cries out, "Courage!"

Let's just stop right there. Instead of saying, "It's Me, guys!" right off the bat, He starts with the word "Courage!"

When you're facing a scary situation, the first word from your Savior is "Courage, girl!" Then He reminds you of who He is. He's the Creator of all, the one who can save you from the circumstance in front of you.

He will teach you to walk on water if you put your trust in Him. Don't wait for a scary situation to test that theory! He has you covered 24-7.

I trust You, Jesus. You're teaching me how to walk above my circumstances. I won't sink with my hand in Yours! Amen.

JESUS REMINDS US THAT ALL THINGS ARE POSSIBLE

*Jesus looked straight at them and answered,
"This is impossible for human beings but not
for God; everything is possible for God."*
MARK 10:27 GNT

What does the word *everything* mean? How are the words *everything* and *things* different? If Jesus had said, "Things are possible for God," you might wonder, *What things?* But He said everything. And everything means, well. . .everything.

A financial nightmare? It's possible for God. A health crisis? That falls in the "everything" category too. A broken relationship? A busted marriage? A wandering child? All everythings.

Nothing is too hard for God. That might be hard to comprehend because you're not Him. But there's not a problem you can name that He can't solve. And because He loves you, you know that He has your back.

All things are possible for Him. And guess what? They're also possible for those who believe.

---

*I'll increase my faith today, Jesus! I will continue to
trust that, with You, all things are possible! Amen.*

JESUS CAME TO SERVE

"For even the Son of Man did not come to be served;
he came to serve and to give his life to redeem many people."

MARK 10:45 GNT

If someone asked, "Do you have a servant's heart?," how would you answer that question? If we want to be like Jesus, we have to excel at serving others.

This concept flies in the face of twenty-first-century living, doesn't it? These days, it's all about putting yourself first. People can be so demanding. If they don't get what they want, they pitch a fit.

Jesus, though? He never put Himself first. He focused on the crippled man in need of healing, the tax collector no one else wanted to hang out with, the prostitute who longed to change her situation.

He not only saw those people, He served those people. He healed, He touched, He fed, He transformed. And He hopes you'll do the same with those you come in contact with.

A life of service is a life like His. What a simple plan for living!

I want to be a servant like You, Jesus. May I turn my
focus from myself and focus on others. Amen.

JESUS WANTS US TO COVER THE GLOBE

He said to them, "Go throughout the whole world and preach the gospel to all people."

MARK 16:15 GNT

The world is filled with billions of people from thousands of different culture groups. Even inside of those culture groups, you find hundreds of belief systems and religions. It's overwhelming if you stop to think about it. Sometimes it can feel like Christians are up against a tsunami of people who don't know Jesus. . .and don't seem to want to know Him.

So, how do we cover the globe? Really, it's simple. When we pour out love—to our brothers and sisters who are different— we are preaching the gospel. Love them like Jesus loved. Treat them the way Jesus treated others. Pray for them the way He calls you to pray.

Take advantage of places like social media to think about the impact you can have as a believer. Speak carefully. Prayerfully. You really can change the world one person at a time.

I want to make an impact on the people of this world, Jesus. Show me how, I pray. Amen.

JESUS ASCENDED TO HEAVEN

After the Lord Jesus had talked with them, he was taken up to heaven and sat at the right side of God.

MARK 16:19 GNT

Imagine you're standing in a field with the Savior. He's already died on the cross and busted loose from the tomb, alive again. You're pretty overwhelmed with all of that. Then, after a few miracles and parting words, He begins to rise into the air, disappearing into the clouds.

Poof. Gone.

If you had any lingering doubts in your mind about the validity of His story, they would fade in that very moment as you witnessed with your own eyes something so incredibly supernatural.

Jesus might have gone back to heaven, but that goodbye wasn't the end of the story. He sent the Comforter, the Holy Spirit, to walk with us every step of the way. In other words, He left. . .but He didn't really leave. He's still right here with us.

What a day that must have been, Jesus! To see You rise into the air, headed home to heaven. What was that like? I'm so grateful You didn't leave us alone. Thank You for sending the Helper! Amen.

JESUS, BORN OF A VIRGIN

The angel said to her, "Don't be afraid, Mary; God has been gracious to you. You will become pregnant and give birth to a son, and you will name him Jesus."

LUKE 1:30–31 GNT

Have you ever wondered why Jesus was born of a virgin? Why not just show up on earth the same way he left. . .floating through the skies? Why come as a baby?

The birth of the Christ child showed the humility of God coming in human form. He was one of us, from the moment of conception in that sweet virgin girl to the moment of His ascension.

Coming from the womb of a virgin, the Savior of the world was undeniably born in the usual way, but His birth was foretold over a thousand years prior.

When the Christ child was born, He fulfilled that prophecy, and nothing has been the same since!

I trust You, Jesus. You're Emmanuel, God with us!
Thank You for coming as a babe in the manger to live
a sinless life and die on a cross for me. Amen.

JESUS, CONCEIVED BY THE SPIRIT

*The angel answered, "The Holy Spirit will come on
you, and God's power will rest upon you. For this
reason the holy child will be called the Son of God."*

LUKE 1:35 GNT

Jesus was conceived by the Spirit of God. No human father was required for His conception. Think about that for a moment. He had an earthly mother but a heavenly Father. He arrived nine months later, fully God, fully man.

Through the generations, people have tried to claim that He must've had an earthly father, that the story of His conception couldn't possibly be true. We know, however, that God doesn't lie. So, the full story of Jesus' birth is biblical truth. You can take it to the bank.

You can trust the Savior, born of a virgin, was conceived by the Spirit of God. He truly is who He claims to be!

You're the only one who ever walked on this earth who didn't have an earthly father, Jesus. You were conceived supernaturally. What a miraculous story! What a miraculous Savior! Amen.

JESUS, HUMBLE BEGINNINGS

And while they were in Bethlehem, the time came for
her to have her baby. She gave birth to her first son,
wrapped him in cloths and laid him in a manger—
there was no room for them to stay in the inn.

LUKE 2:6–7 GNT

Jesus' birth was prophesied years in advance, including the location:
Bethlehem.

Jesus had humble beginnings. He was born in a lowly stable,
surrounded by sheep and cattle. The King of kings wasn't born in a
palace. He didn't come in with fanfare and shouting. A quiet night
in Bethlehem with the lowing of cattle was the setting for His birth.

Maybe you know what it means to have a humble birth. Perhaps
you didn't come from an affluent home or a family of means. You've
always felt "less than."

It's time to change your perspective, girl! You're a child of the
Most High God, born to royalty. Don't let your birth define you.
Jesus surely didn't! He went on to save the world, after all!

I'm not a product of my environment, Lord. I see that
now. You created me to do great things for You, no
matter how humble my beginnings! Amen.

JESUS, BELOVED SON OF GOD

*Now when all the people were baptized, and when Jesus
also had been baptized and was praying, the heavens
were opened, and the Holy Spirit descended on him in
bodily form, like a dove; and a voice came from heaven,
"You are my beloved Son; with you I am well pleased."*
LUKE 3:21–22 ESV

What does it mean to be a beloved child? If you're a parent, no
doubt you've experienced a supernatural love for your little ones.
They wrap themselves around your heart and don't let go. That
kind of love is God-breathed, isn't it?

Jesus was deeply loved by His Father. Isn't it wonderful that
God took the time to include the words "You are my beloved Son;
with you I am well pleased"?

Sometimes kiddos need that kind of encouragement. Let's face
it: sometimes adults need that kind of encouragement. Knowing
you're loved by your Father can give you the courage and tenacity
to keep going, even when you don't feel like it.

Today, spend time loving on the little ones in your life. Offer
words of encouragement and praise, and watch as their little
faces glow!

*Thank You for loving us—Your kids—so much, Lord!
Show me how to love as You do. Amen.*

JESUS, TEMPTED IN EVERY WAY

*And Jesus, full of the Holy Spirit, returned from the Jordan
and was led by the Spirit in the wilderness for forty days,
being tempted by the devil. And he ate nothing during
those days. And when they were ended, he was hungry.*

LUKE 4:1–2 ESV

Have you ever faced a temptation that was too much to bear?
Maybe you promised yourself that you wouldn't eat that slice of
cake. . .then ate two.

Or maybe you made up your mind you wouldn't spend so
much money but then gave in and purchased that cute shirt you
saw at the mall.

These things happen. We get tempted, we give in, we beg God
for forgiveness and pledge not to do it again. Then (usually) we
fall into the same traps.

Jesus knew what it was like to be tempted. He was tempted by
the devil during His forty days in the wilderness. The enemy tried
to trap Him several times, but Jesus rose above the temptations.

You can rise above them too. Even the ones that plague you
most. When you're full of the Spirit of God, you have the power
to say, "No!"

---

*I can say no with Your help, Jesus. You showed me how to rise
above my temptations. I want to be more like You. Amen.*

JESUS, SEEKER OF SINNERS

*"I have not come to call the righteous
but sinners to repentance."*
LUKE 5:32 ESV

It's funny, isn't it? People say things like "I can't go to church because I'm such a bad sinner." Or maybe they say, "I can't get my act together, so God won't take me like I am."

Looking back over the words of Jesus, it's clear to see that He didn't come for the saints. He came for the sinners. He didn't say, "Clean up your act and come to Me." He said (and continues to say), "Come to Me as you are, and I'll shower you with My love."

He will, you know. No matter what you've done. No matter where you've been. No matter the lack. He will accept you, love you, and sweep you into His kingdom with as much passion as He would welcome anyone else.

You are loved.

---

*You came for people like me, Jesus.
I'm so grateful to be Yours! Amen.*

JESUS CALLS US BLESSED

"Blessed are you when people hate you and when they exclude you and revile you and spurn your name as evil, on account of the Son of Man!"

LUKE 6:22 ESV

You've probably figured this out by now, but not everyone is going to love you. For that matter, not everyone is going to like you. It might not make much sense to you at times. After all, you're pretty lovable. And it hurts when they don't see the real you.

Take a look at today's verse. Jesus understood what it felt like to be unloved. He understood the pain of exclusion, of feeling left out. Worse still, He understood what it was like to be reviled. Hated.

Ugh. It's awful to know that people feel that way about you, isn't it? But Jesus takes the conversation a step further. He says that you are blessed when people are their cruelest. Take heart in that, friend.

It hurts when others aren't kind to me, Jesus, but You understand and You call me blessed. Thank You for caring so much. Amen.

JESUS DEFINES THE LEAST AND GREATEST

*But Jesus, knowing the reasoning of their hearts, took
a child and put him by his side and said to them,
"Whoever receives this child in my name receives me,
and whoever receives me receives him who sent me. For
he who is least among you all is the one who is great."*

LUKE 9:47–48 ESV

What a fascinating lesson Jesus was attempting to teach here. He took a child, an innocent little one, and said, "Whoever receives this little child in My name receives Me, and whoever receives Me receives Him who sent Me."

What do you suppose He meant by that?

In a patriarchal society, children were (perhaps) low rungs on the totem pole. But the "least" among them (the children) were greatest in His eyes.

Jesus wants us to open our eyes to the people around us. That homeless person on the street corner. That checker in the grocery store. That man mowing your neighbor's yard. They are all the greatest in God's eyes.

---

*Thank You for the reminder that the least are really the greatest,
Lord. May I never forget that all people have value. Amen.*

JESUS CAME FOR THE LOST

"For the Son of Man came to seek and to save the lost."
Luke 19:10 esv

Have you ever wondered why Jesus left heaven and came to earth? He came to find those who were lost.

Remember what it was like as a child to play hide-and-seek? Which was more fun, to be the one missing or the one on the prowl? There's something very exciting about finding the lost ones and bringing them to the light.

Jesus lived to find those who needed light. And He wasn't biased in who He found. Young, old, rich, poor. . .He was after every heart.

He's still after every heart, and He's hoping you will be too. If you want to be like Jesus, begin your quest to seek the lost.

I want to be like You, Jesus. May the lost be found, and may I play a role in bringing them into the light. Amen.

JESUS FACED DEATH

Then Jesus, calling out with a loud voice, said,
"Father, into your hands I commit my spirit!"
And having said this he breathed his last.

LUKE 23:46 ESV

Jesus was born to die. Maybe you read that and think, *Same with me!* Life is short, after all. We have our time on planet Earth, and then we transition to heaven.

The story of Jesus was considerably different from ours in that He specifically came to die for us. His death had an eternal purpose. And even in the very moment of His death, He cried out, "Father, I'm Yours! Have My spirit!"

He exhibited faith even in the midst of His worst challenge.

We'll all transition to heaven one day. May we face that transition with the faith and purpose of our Savior, who led the way with His final words.

I want to have faith even when facing the ultimate
challenges, Lord. Thank You for leading the way and
showing me how to face the hard things. Amen.

JESUS, RESURRECTED SAVIOR

"He is not here, but has risen. Remember how he told you, while he was still in Galilee, that the Son of Man must be delivered into the hands of sinful men and be crucified and on the third day rise."

LUKE 24:6–7 ESV

"He's not here. He has risen!"

Can you imagine hearing those words from the perspective of the women at the tomb? They saw Jesus murdered. They watched Him die. They looked on as His body was carried to the tomb and the stone was rolled in front of it, sealing Him in.

Now, three days later. . . "He is not here."

What? Where did He go?

The angel answered the question: "He has risen. Remember. . .He told you this was going to happen!"

Jesus had predicted both His death and resurrection, but in the chaos of the events that took place on that infamous week, His followers were lost and confused.

Jesus rose again. And nothing has been the same since.

Thank You for the power of Your resurrection, Jesus! Amen.

JESUS IS THE WORD

In the beginning was the Word, and the Word was with God,
and the Word was God. He was in the beginning with God.

JOHN 1:1–2 ESV

Are there people in your life that you trust implicitly? Maybe you have a good friend who always speaks the truth. You know that her word is trustworthy.

Jesus has always been trustworthy. He was there in the beginning. The Word was with God, and the Word was God. So, when the words "Let there be light!" were spoken, it all came from Him.

It might be hard to wrap your mind around all of that, but here's the truth: He's always been and He always will be. And the words of Jesus—either written in the Bible or on your heart—are true. You can take Him at His word not just now but always.

Check out the "written in red" verses in the Bible. Those are His words to you.

I will take You at Your word, Jesus! If you said it, I believe it. I trust the letters in red. Thank You for writing them on my heart! Amen.

JESUS, MAKER OF ALL

He was in the beginning with God. All things were made through him, and without him was not any thing made that was made. In him was life, and the life was the light of men. The light shines in the darkness, and the darkness has not overcome it.

JOHN 1:2–5 ESV

Jesus was in the beginning with God. He saw it all. He heard it all. He made it all.

This boggles the mind until you realize that the Father and the Son are one and the same. Nothing came to being without Jesus' input. Life. Light. Creation. Everything!

Jesus is just as active in His creation today as He was when Adam first walked in the garden. He cares as much about you as He cared about Adam. (Crazy to think about, right?)

You were made by Him, through Him, and for Him. And He wants you to be a light that shines in the darkness, even in these perilous times. You were created for this, woman of God!

It's not always easy to be a light in the darkness, until I remember that You created me for this time and this purpose. Thank You, my maker, for being actively engaged in my life so that I can be more effective for You. Amen.

THE WORLD DIDN'T KNOW HIM

He was in the world, and the world was made through him, yet the world did not know him.

JOHN 1:10 ESV

Have you ever felt like people just didn't get you? Maybe you've been through seasons of feeling like you don't fit in. You can't find your place. No one seems to really know the real you.

Congratulations! If you feel like this, you're more like Jesus than you know. He came to this world—a world He created, by the way—and the world didn't know Him. The very people He breathed to life didn't seem to have a clue who He was. Can you imagine?

The next time you're feeling "unknown," remember that there is one who knows you better than anyone else. Jesus, the one who formed you inside and out, knows every intricate part of you. He gets you. He loves you. And He plans to stay with you for all your days.

Thank You for knowing me so intimately, Jesus. When no one else gets me, You do. I'm so grateful for Your love. Amen.

JESUS, REJECTED BY HIS OWN

He came to his own, and his own people did not receive him.
JOHN 1:11 ESV

There's nothing worse than being hurt by the very people you love the most, the ones you thought you could trust. It stinks, right? When you face rejection at the hands of those in your inner circle, the pain can be unfathomable.

Jesus understands. He went through this with the Jewish people. Many of them didn't believe that He was the Messiah, the Son of God. They rejected Him and His message. Can you imagine the pain He must have experienced as the very ones He came to save turned away from Him?

You'll go through seasons of rejection, but you will never be alone. He's right there, feeling it all with you.

Thank You for sticking with me, Jesus. . .for never ever rejecting me or turning me away. I'm always safe with You and loved by You. Amen.

JESUS TOOK ON FLESH

And the Word became flesh and dwelt among us,
and we have seen his glory, glory as of the only
Son from the Father, full of grace and truth.
JOHN 1:14 ESV

Imagine you were raised in a castle, the daughter of a king. Now imagine you decided to give all of that up to live among the poor, tending to their needs and making sure they had everything they needed. What a difference between those two worlds!

Jesus lived in a state of perfection in heaven. Can you envision the bliss He must have experienced? And yet, He chose to wrap Himself in flesh and come to this broken, chaotic world for us. He walked away from a life of royalty to a life where he owned no home, had no place to lay His head, and spent most days dealing with people who questioned His integrity.

We see glimpses of heaven when we see Jesus. And we see the love of one who would give up everything for those He loves.

Thank You for loving me so much that You came, Jesus. You wrapped Yourself in flesh and walked among us, ready to love in spite of our brokenness. How grateful I am! Amen.

JESUS, THE LAMB OF GOD

The next day he saw Jesus coming toward him, and said, "Behold, the Lamb of God, who takes away the sin of the world!"

John 1:29 esv

Why do you suppose Jesus is repeatedly referred to as the lamb of God?

In biblical days, a spotless lamb was used as a sacrifice to atone for the sins of the people. Once the high priest shed the blood of the lamb, the atonement was made on behalf of the people. Their sins were rolled back.

Jesus was the ultimate spotless lamb. He laid down His life, as a lamb led to the slaughter. He never complained about His sacrifice. He simply gave Himself, knowing that His offering would change (literally) everything for mankind.

Today, as you ponder that sacrifice, take the time to thank Him for what He did for you. Jesus—the spotless lamb—gave His all so that you could have eternal life.

Jesus, I'm so grateful to You, the spotless lamb. Thank You for offering Yourself as a sacrifice for all. Amen.

JESUS BAPTIZES WITH THE SPIRIT

"I myself did not know him, but he who sent me to baptize with water said to me, 'He on whom you see the Spirit descend and remain, this is he who baptizes with the Holy Spirit.'"

JOHN 1:33 ESV

Jesus' baptism was predicted. John knew that the one on whom the Spirit descended would be the true baptizer. Jesus wouldn't baptize people with water. He promised to baptize (immerse) people with the Spirit.

So, what does it mean to be immersed with the Spirit of God? To be Spirit-controlled means that you release every area of your life to His control. You expect and receive the fruit of the Spirit—love, joy, peace, patience, kindness, goodness, faithfulness, gentleness, and self-control. You expect and receive specific gifts of the Spirit, the ones that God has ordained for you. You can then operate in the gifts and fruit of the Spirit to have the most productive and healthy life while drawing others to Him.

Today, ask for a fresh immersion in the Spirit of God. He will fill you to overflowing!

Thank You for Your Spirit, God! Fill me to the top, I pray. Amen.

JESUS PERFORMED SIGNS AND WONDERS

Now when he was in Jerusalem at the Passover Feast, many believed in his name when they saw the signs that he was doing.

JOHN 2:23 ESV

Jesus has always been in the miracle-working business. He was there in the beginning, speaking the world into existence. Miraculous! During His ministry years, He gave sight to blind eyes and brought health and hope to the sick.

And here's the thing—He's still performing miracles today. That near accident that didn't take place. That cancer diagnosis that ended better than expected. That broken relationship that came together in the end. . .He's front and center in all of it.

Don't stop praying and believing for miracles. No matter what you're up against today, He's still a miracle-working God, and He wants the best for you.

I'm so glad You're a miracle-working God! No matter what I'm facing, I know I can ask for Your best for my situation. Amen.

JESUS SPEAKS OF REBIRTH

Jesus answered him, "Truly, truly, I say to you, unless one is born again he cannot see the kingdom of God."

JOHN 3:3 ESV

Jesus spoke a consistent message of rebirth. Being "born again" was a hot topic for Him. Why do you suppose He kept driving home this point?

He understood what mankind did not: one birth experience wasn't enough. To experience eternal life, one has to be born a second time, of the Spirit of God.

Have you offered your heart to Jesus? Are you born again? Have you been born of the Spirit? If not, then this is your day. Ask Jesus to come and live in your heart. Watch your life, your situation, be reborn. He can bring beauty from the ashes of your life, no matter what you're walking through at this very moment.

Best of all, the born again experience assures you a place in heaven for all eternity. There, all the problems of this life will grow strangely dim, as the old hymn says.

Thank You for new birth, Jesus! You came to give life, and abundant life at that! I'm so grateful to be reborn. Amen.

FOR GOD SO LOVED THE WORLD

"For God so loved the world, that he gave his only Son, that whoever believes in him should not perish but have eternal life."

JOHN 3:16 ESV

If there's one key takeaway from the life of Jesus, it's this: when you love, you give.

Jesus loved mankind so much that He gave. He gave His life. He gave miracles. He gave love. He gave encouragement. He gave fishing lessons. He gave grace.

He gave. And He wants us to give too.

What's in your goodie bag today? What do you have to give away? Love? Joy? Peace? Hope? Grace? Goodness? Gentleness? Kindness? There's always something tucked away that you can give others.

Be like Jesus. Give it away, even when you don't feel like it.

Thank You for leading by example, Jesus. You gave it all away so that I could live. Teach me how to give as You do. Amen.

JESUS EXPLAINS THE WORK OF GOD

*Jesus answered them, "This is the work of God,
that you believe in him whom he has sent."*

JOHN 6:29 ESV

Jesus came to fulfill a mandate. He had work to do. His work included sharing the gospel message and spreading the news that God was intimately and passionately in love with humanity.

You have work to do too. God has given you special gifts to share with others. You might have particular talents or abilities that could be usable to the kingdom of God. Or you might be someone who says, "Me? I have talents?"

Oh, you do! He gifted every woman uniquely so that she could touch humanity in her own special way.

Be like Jesus. Do the work. Leave an imprint on this world.

---

*Show me how to do the best work for You,
Jesus. I want to leave an imprint! Amen.*

JESUS, LIVING BREAD

"I am the living bread that came down from heaven. If anyone eats of this bread, he will live forever. And the bread that I will give for the life of the world is my flesh."
JOHN 6:51 ESV

Imagine you saw a commercial for a new food product, one you could eat that would leave you feeling satisfied forever. Would you rush to the store and buy it? Now imagine that food product was absolutely free, though it cost the manufacturer greatly. No doubt you would appreciate it even more!

Jesus called Himself the living bread. He made what must have seemed like an outlandish promise when He said, "If anyone eats of this bread, he will live forever."

That's a life-changing bread! You'll never go hungry with a bread like that. And yes, it cost the manufacturer a great deal. In this case, the promise cost our Savior His very life. What a promise! What a Savior!

Jesus, thank You for being my living bread. Thank You for Your body, which was broken for me. I'll partake and never go hungry again! Amen.

JESUS, SENT BY THE FATHER

"As the living Father sent me, and I live because of the Father,
so whoever feeds on me, he also will live because of me."

John 6:57 esv

Jesus was sent on a mission by His Father. Think about that for a moment. When the Father gave Him His marching orders, the Son could have said, "Nope. I don't think so. That sounds like too much trouble!" But He didn't. Jesus fully cooperated with His Father's plan.

How do you respond when God gives you marching orders? Do you cooperate or stomp your foot? Sometimes, especially when the tasks seem hard, we rebel. We say, "Nope. Not me. Not this time. Choose someone else."

God doesn't want to choose someone else. He picked you for this task. And He's hoping you'll carry through.

What are you trying to weasel out of today? Deep breath, girl. You can do this.

I'll admit it, Jesus. . .I don't always like to follow Your plan. Sometimes I get overwhelmed. It seems too hard, too uncomfortable. I feel like You ask a lot of me (just keeping it real). But You did the hardest thing of all. Help me to learn from You. Amen.

JESUS, CONVEYER OF GOD'S MESSAGE

Jesus said to them, "What I teach is not Mine. It is from God Who sent Me."

JOHN 7:16 NLV

Have you ever been asked to teach someone else's material? Maybe you're teaching a Bible study or class at school, and the material isn't yours. But there you are, standing in front of your students, hoping you can do justice to what you've been given to teach.

Jesus came with God's material. God's lesson. And guess what? That's the same lesson you're here to teach. Oh, it's tempting to come up with your own stuff, to add your own twist. But the Bible doesn't really need any twisting. (In fact, it's highly frowned upon!)

God's Word is filled with lovely lessons, and you're the perfect person to convey them to the folks in your circle. God picked you, and He picked the subject matter. So live and love according to His Word, and you'll do just fine!

I'll teach Your Word, Jesus. You have the best lessons of all. Amen.

JESUS UNDERSTOOD THE TIMELINE

Jesus said to them, "I will be with you a little while yet. Then I will go back to Him Who sent Me."
JOHN 7:33 NLV

Have you ever questioned God's timeline? It happens to a lot of us! He asks us to wait, and we get fidgety. Our patience grows thin. We give up. We forget His promises. We forget all of the times He's come through for us in the past.

When Jesus came from heaven to earth, He understood His Father's timeline. He had that advantage. You don't know God's timeline, but you can trust that His timing is perfect, even when it seems like He's lagging behind. God is never tardy. Even in the eleventh hour, He is still plotting your victory! He will come through for you.

I'll wait on You, Jesus. You understand the timeline.
I don't always feel like being patient, but You're
showing me how to wait on You. Amen.

JESUS OFFERS LIVING WATER

*It was the last and great day of the religious gathering.
Jesus stood up and spoke with a loud voice, "If anyone
is thirsty, let him come to Me and drink."*

John 7:37 nlv

Picture yourself walking across the Sahara. You're parched and dry. Your lips are cracked. Then, up ahead, an oasis! You stop for a long drink of the refreshing water, then set out on your way again. An hour later, guess what? You're thirsty once again. So this time, you reach for your water bottle, which you filled back at the oasis.

That might seem like a silly illustration, but that's what it's like to come to Jesus, the living water. You can drink from that well and fill your bottle to overflowing. Best of all, it will never run dry! He will satisfy you all the days of your life!

*Today I feel parched and dry, Jesus. I come to You thirsty
and ready to drink from the living fountain, the one that
will satisfy me 24-7 for the rest of my life. Amen.*

JESUS, LIGHT OF THE WORLD

Jesus spoke to all the people, saying, "I am the Light of the world. Anyone who follows Me will not walk in darkness. He will have the Light of Life."

JOHN 8:12 NLV

If you've ever been through a terrible storm and lost power even for a few hours, you know how difficult it can be maneuvering in the dark.

The Bible calls Jesus "the light of the world." If you really dig deep in the scriptures, you'll see the earth described as being cloaked in darkness before He came in flesh. The reference is to spiritual darkness, of course. The sun still rose and set every day. The people could see the way to get from place to place. But spiritually, they were completely in the dark.

Many today are in the darkness simply because they haven't accepted the light of Christ into their lives. You can be a light, shining the way. Lead them to Him, and they'll never walk in darkness again!

Jesus, You are the light. This world needs You as much as ever! So many are staggering around in darkness, spiritually speaking. Show me how to shine brightly for You. Amen.

JESUS SETS US FREE. . .INDEED!

"So if the Son makes you free, you will be free for sure."
JOHN 8:36 NLV

Have you ever answered someone's question and then added the words *for sure!* at the end? The "for sure" is really just your way of saying "You can take this to the bank."

Jesus died on the cross to purchase salvation for all who would place their trust in Him. If you've given Him your heart (you have, haven't you?), then salvation is yours. You've been set free from the bondages of yesterday, the things that used to plague you. And Jesus follows up this truth with an emphasis on the words *for sure*.

For sure, you've been set free. There's no need to go backward. There's no need to get hung up on guilt or shame. Yesterday is in the past. Today is a new day.

For sure.

Jesus! Thank You. . .for sure! I'm so grateful yesterday is behind me and I'm free to move forward with Your hand in mine. Amen.

JESUS, OUR DOOR

*"I am the Door. Anyone who goes in through
Me will be saved from the punishment of sin.
He will go in and out and find food."*

JOHN 10:9 NLV

Imagine you are in a rotunda, a completely rounded room with no windows. You walk in, and the door closes. . .then disappears. You turn in circles, trying to get your bearings, but the door is cleverly hidden away in the texture of the wall, and you can't make it out.

After a while, you start to feel panicked. Trapped! No way out!

That's kind of how life feels sometimes. You get into situations with no windows and no doors. You feel stuck.

Jesus is your door, even in the hardest windowless situations. He's the way out. He's the way through. He's the only one who can rescue you and set you free. Today, wait no longer. Use the door, girl!

---

*You're my way out, Jesus! You have saved me and given
me a doorway to good things. I'm so grateful. Amen.*

JESUS, ONE WITH THE FATHER

"I give them life that lasts forever. They will never be punished. No one is able to take them out of My hand. My Father Who gave them to Me is greater than all. No one is able to take them out of My Father's hand. My Father and I are one!"

JOHN 10:28–30 NLV

Jesus was one with the Father. Even though He came in flesh, they still maintained their "oneness" status.

Have you ever been one with someone? Maybe a spouse? Or a child? Or a group of fellow believers?

Walking in unity (oneness) is key. There's power in numbers, after all. More than anything, Jesus wants you to be one with Him. Today, if you find yourself distanced from your Savior, recommit yourself to unity with Him. Give Him your heart—fully, completely, and unreservedly.

I want to be one with You, Jesus. Draw me close, I pray. Amen.

JESUS WANTS US TO BELIEVE

*Jesus said to her, "Did I not say that if you would believe,
you would see the shining-greatness of God?"*

JOHN 11:40 NLV

"Didn't I tell you?" Maybe you've heard those words a time or two in your life. Maybe you've spoken them to a child or friend.

"Didn't I tell you?" is a nicer way of saying "I told you so!" In this verse, Jesus is kind of saying "I told you so!" to His followers. He's reminding them of something He's already spoken in the past, reiterating that they will eventually see the shining-greatness of God if they just believe.

When we're walking through valleys, it's not easy to remember that shining-greatness is ahead of us. We just see shadows and feel fear. But if Jesus felt strongly enough about it to add an "I told you so," maybe we'd better sit up and pay attention.

If you believe, breakthrough is coming. He said it. You can believe it.

---

*I won't give up when the shadows fall, Jesus. You tell me that
I will see breakthrough if I will just believe. Today, I choose
to do that, despite any signs to the contrary. Amen.*

JESUS, TEACHER AND LORD

"You call Me Teacher and Lord. You are
right because that is what I am."

John 13:13 nlv

These days, titles seem to be more important than ever. People are very specific about how they want to be addressed, what they want to be called.

In Jesus' day, leaders were always addressed with respect and dignity. To some, Jesus was not who He said He was. They refused to acknowledge His divinity. To others, He was both teacher and Lord.

We tend to speak what we believe, so it's easy to call Him "Lord" when you've made Him Lord of your life. It's easy to call Him "teacher" when you're constantly in His Word, learning all He has for you.

Want success to come? Make Him Lord of your life, and then become a ready student of His Word. Be open to the movement of His Spirit, and watch as He leads You along His path.

Lord, You are both teacher and Lord in my life.
I could never make it without You! Amen.

JESUS INSTRUCTS US TO WASH FEET

"I am your Teacher and Lord. I have washed your feet. You should wash each other's feet also."

JOHN 13:14 NLV

When you think of washing someone else's feet, what thoughts go through your mind? Does the idea sound icky to you? Or do you see it as a humbling but beautiful act?

In biblical days, people traveled long, hot miles in sandals. When they arrived at their destination, their feet were dirty. Caked. It wasn't unusual to offer them water to bathe their feet as they entered the home.

This act of submission is a simple way of saying, "I care about you. I appreciate you. You've made a difference in my life, and you are worthy of tender loving care." It doesn't have to be a physical act of foot washing either. Love that hard-to-love neighbor. Speak kind words to the child who smarts off to you. Wash the feet of that coworker who speaks so abrasively. As you do so, you will become more like Jesus.

---

*Show me how to wash feet today, Jesus.
I want to be more like You. Amen.*

JESUS, OWNER OF A BIG HOUSE

"There is more than enough room in my Father's home. If this were not so, would I have told you that I am going to prepare a place for you?"

JOHN 14:2 NLT

Have you ever wished you lived in a bigger house? Maybe you feel crammed in without adequate cabinet or closet space. Maybe people are doubled up in the bedrooms out of necessity. It happens.

The day is coming when you'll experience the biggest house of all. Jesus spoke of it in this verse from John 14. Some Bible versions refer to it as a mansion. It's a big, big house—plenty big enough for everyone to spread out and still have room.

What do you think Jesus was saying here? He's letting us know that there's room in the kingdom of God for all who would come. It won't be standing room only in His house. He's preparing a place for us even now. A big, big place.

Thank You for making room for all of us, Jesus! I can't wait to spend eternity in that big, big house. . .with You! Amen.

KNOW JESUS, KNOW THE FATHER

"If you had really known me, you would know who my Father is. From now on, you do know him and have seen him!"

John 14:7 NLT

Have you ever met someone who looked and acted so much like one of their parents that you couldn't help but laugh? It happens!

We reflect those we're related to, whether we want to admit it or not. We often look like them, speak like them, and act like them.

Jesus looked like His Father too. He made a pretty bold statement when He said, "Know Me, know the Father." These words didn't sit well with the naysayers. They didn't want to believe He was the Son of God. But Jesus wasn't lying! When you come to know Him, you really are getting to know the Father. In this case, "like Father, like Son" is definitely true!

I want to know You more, Jesus. And I realize that, in knowing You, I'm also getting to know my heavenly Father. When I see You, I see Him. What a revelation! Amen.

JESUS WANTS US TO ASK IN HIS NAME

"You can ask for anything in my name, and I will do it, so that the Son can bring glory to the Father."
JOHN 14:13 NLT

Imagine you're standing at a locked door, and you read a nearby sign: SPEAK THE WORD *OPEN!* AND THE DOOR WILL OPEN. What would you do? You'd speak the word *OPEN!* of course!

That's kind of how it is when you invoke the name of Jesus into your situation. Closed doors, even those that were slammed shut, have to open in His name. Demons tremble at that name. Mountains are cast into the sea. Situations change.

Ask in His name. No matter what you're going through today, no matter how many times you've experienced disappointment, ask again. Invoke that holy, precious name. Jesus moves on your behalf to bring glory to His Father!

Jesus, today I speak Your name over my situation.
Work miracles, I pray, in Jesus' name! Amen.

JESUS WANTS OBEDIENCE

"If you love me, obey my commandments."

JOHN 14:15 NLT

Obedience.

What is it about this word that makes us want to turn and run in the opposite direction? We say we want to do what God expects from us, until He makes it plain what He expects from us. Then suddenly, a rebellious streak rises. We don't want to do it. We feel like we shouldn't have to.

That same rebellious streak rose in Adam and Eve, and mankind is still paying a terrible price for it. Sometimes rebellion has consequences with ripple effects that hurt your family, friends, and other loved ones.

Today, pray for an obedient heart, one that says yes to God no matter the question. Obedience is a true act of faith, but God will help you each step of the way.

I give my heart and my will to You afresh today, Jesus. I want what You want. May I chase after obedience all the days of my life. Amen.

JESUS WILL NEVER ABANDON US

"No, I will not abandon you as orphans—I will come to you."
JOHN 14:18 NLT

No doubt you've heard stories of babies being left on doorsteps. Desperate mothers and fathers set their children down and walk away, most hoping the baby will have a far better life on the other side of this decision.

A parentless child has a hard time feeling loved and accepted. Only when he is adopted into a loving family can healing come.

Perhaps this is why Jesus uses this particular verbiage when talking about His relationship with us. He'll never leave us feeling abandoned on a doorstep. He wants us to know we're safe and secure as a part of His family. And He drives home the point that He will come to us. He's the Father, sweeping us into His arms when we're at our most vulnerable.

You can trust Him today, no matter what you're facing.

Thank You for not abandoning me, Jesus.
I'm so happy to be safe with You. Amen.

JESUS SPEAKS OF AN ADVOCATE

"But when the Father sends the Advocate as my representative—that is, the Holy Spirit—he will teach you everything and will remind you of everything I have told you."
JOHN 14:26 NLT

Are you one of the millions who struggles with a learning disability? Some people really struggle to learn until techniques are adjusted. Even then, many have a hard time catching on to concepts.

No matter how deep your learning struggles, Jesus has the answer. He sent the Holy Spirit not just as a comforter but to teach and train us. He can impress biblical concepts on your heart and teach you things that can only be learned by the Spirit. You don't need a college degree. On the contrary, you'll need to push conventional learning styles aside and depend on the supernatural.

The Spirit of God will train you to do all that God has called you to do. Don't stress. Don't worry that you're not capable. With His help, you will be.

I will rely on You, my teacher! Thank You, Lord, for leading me by Your Spirit! Amen.

JESUS, THE VINE

"Yes, I am the vine; you are the branches. Those who remain in me, and I in them, will produce much fruit. For apart from me you can do nothing."

JOHN 15:5 NLT

In the autumn, leaves begin to tumble from the trees. They land on the ground below and begin the death process. Apart from the life of the tree, they cannot sustain themselves.

The same is true for you. Apart from the life-giving tree (Jesus), you will never make it on your own. Oh, you can try, but you're just a withered little leaf on the ground instead of a lush, green, healthy one.

Cling to the vine. Stick with Him even when the world tries to pull you away. Hang tight even when you feel like giving up. Remain in Him even when He's not moving as fast as you might've hoped.

You'll never be sorry for sticking with Jesus, but you'll pay a heavy price if you don't.

I'll cling to You, Jesus. You are my true vine. With You, I can do anything, so I will hang tight. Amen.

REMAIN IN HIM

"But if you remain in me and my words remain in you, you may ask for anything you want, and it will be granted!"

JOHN 15:7 NLT

Have you ever been in a relationship where the other person refused to stick around? Maybe as a child you experienced an absent parent—an alcoholic who couldn't put down the bottle, or a parent who was so focused on their job that they couldn't remember the family.

Staying in relationship takes dedication. Work. It's not always easy, but it's always worth the effort.

Jesus wants you to stay in relationship with Him. Keep His words planted deep in your heart. When you're walking that closely with Him, where you know His thoughts, His heart, then totally trust Him. That sort of trust sparks faith. You can ask for anything, and He will spring to action! He loves you that much.

I will remain in You, Jesus. I know You're planning to stick around, and I will too. Thank You for never giving up on me. I know I can count on You no matter what things look like. Amen.

JESUS LEADS BY EXAMPLE

"When you obey my commandments, you remain in my love, just as I obey my Father's commandments and remain in his love."

JOHN 15:10 NLT

Imagine you were hired at a new company but had no idea what your job description entailed. No one guided you. No one advised you. No one gave you marching orders. You were simply ushered in the door and placed in a cubicle.

You wouldn't last very long, would you? You need leadership. You need guidance. You need examples so that you know what to do.

Jesus led by example. He came. He loved. He shared. He healed. He prayed. He cared. He poured Himself out for others. He fed the hungry, gave drink to the thirsty, encouraged those who felt they were worthless.

Jesus didn't set you in a cubicle to ponder your role on this planet. Be like Him. Follow His lead. You'll be a world changer if you do!

I'll follow Your example, Jesus. I'll love as You love, care as You care, and speak words of love over all I meet. Amen.

JESUS, JOY-GIVER

*"I have told you these things so that you will be
filled with my joy. Yes, your joy will overflow!"*

JOHN 15:11 NLT

If you had a meter to measure your joy level, what would the meter
register right now? Would it be half full? Three-quarters? Or would
it be dipping near the empty mark?

Jesus made an interesting statement to His followers. He said,
"I have told you these things so that you will be filled with my joy."

You know how it goes. When you're in a low place and someone
speaks words of encouragement, they light a spark of hope in you.
The Bible is filled with so many sparks that it can set your heart
ablaze, no matter what you're going through.

Be filled with joy today. Allow your joy meter to register hope,
peace, comfort, and life. May your joy overflow, no matter what
your circumstances might dictate. Jesus can fill you to the very top.

---

*My joy meter is full today, Jesus! You've given me all I need
and more! You continue to pour out joy even on the hardest
of days. I'm so grateful for Your encouragement. Amen.*

JESUS WANTS US TO LOVE AS HE LOVES

"My command is this: Love each other as I have loved you."
JOHN 15:12 NIV

It's one thing to love people. It's another to love them the way Christ does.

His love is unconditional. It's relentless. It pursues those who don't care to be pursued. It cuts through channels of darkness and dips into the lowest valleys. It climbs great heights to locate its intended.

Christ's love never fails. No matter how awkward, painful, or hopeless your situation, His love sees beyond today. It sees all the way to eternity, where the author of love waits with open arms.

Christ's love transcends situations, brokenness, and circumstance.

His love is life, and it's a life He longs for us to share with others. If you want to be like Jesus, love as He loves.

I'll do my best to love the way You've loved me, Jesus! It won't always be easy, but with Your help, it is possible. Amen.

JESUS UNDERSTANDS THE CRUELTY OF THE WORLD

"If the world hates you, keep in mind that it hated me first."
John 15:18 niv

Have you ever felt like you couldn't catch a break? Like everyone and everything in the world was against you? We all go through seasons like that, don't we? When we're facing enemies—both seen and unseen—it can be hard to keep things in perspective. We often feel we'll never have allies. We develop an "us against the world" mentality.

Remember to keep Jesus in your "us." Together, you are a force to be reckoned with. And also remember that He gets it. He understands what it's like to be "us against the world." In His case, though, it was "us *for* the world."

In spite of all that came against Him, Jesus gave Himself willingly. He understood the cruelty of those He was giving His life for, but He gave it anyway.

May I be more like You, Jesus. Even when others turn on me, show me how to love the way You do. Amen.

JESUS WAS SENT BY GOD

*"Now this is eternal life: that they know you, the only
true God, and Jesus Christ, whom you have sent."*
JOHN 17:3 NIV

These are crazy times we're living in. No doubt you sometimes feel like Daniel being thrown in the lions' den. The world can be brutal. People can be cruel. And it's hard to know which way to go when the roar of iniquity is so loud in your ears.

Figuring out your next move—which way to go, whom to trust—is only possible if you remember who is sending you. In the same way that God the Father sent God the Son into the world, He's also sending you.

New Testament scriptures are filled with confirmation that God's plan for the church is to send them out as sheep among wolves. That's kind of a terrifying image, if you think about it. But the point of the sending isn't to see the sheep slaughtered. It's to see them convert the wolves—to see them miraculously delivered and set free so that they can live in peace.

Deep breath. God's sending you. He has big plans for you. With His help, you can do this.

---

*I trust You, Lord. You've called me to do great things for
You. My knees are knocking, but here I go! Amen.*

JESUS FACED DEATH

When he had received the drink, Jesus said, "It is finished."
With that, he bowed his head and gave up his spirit.

JOHN 19:30 NIV

We were all born to die. These human bodies aren't meant to last forever. They age and eventually wear down. And at some point in our lives, we must make peace with the notion that we have to be ready for heaven.

Death isn't something we like to think about, especially when we're young. The older we get, though, the more we have to face it. Parents pass away. Friends die. Loved ones transition to heaven. And the very thing we used to fight when we were younger begins to hold more appeal. We begin to long for heaven.

Jesus faced death. He bowed His head and gave up His Spirit. Even He had to make the transition. And look at the glory on the other side of that story! He rose again!

You will rise too. You'll spend eternity in heaven with the one who gave you life. There's joy on the other side.

I will not fear death, Lord. One day I will
spend eternity with You. Amen.

JESUS IS SENDING US OUT

Again Jesus said, "Peace be with you! As the Father has sent me, I am sending you."
JOHN 20:21 NIV

If you've ever been in the military, you know what it's like to receive your marching orders. And when our servicemen and servicewomen are "called up," they load their gear, hop on a plane, and head off to the battle. There's no looking back. There's no "I don't think I'd like to go this time, thanks." You get on the plane and you go, your eye on the job ahead of you.

That's what it's like when you're in God's army. He has big work for you. There will be training, and it's not always easy. There will be specific calls, and your response is key. There will be battles, but with His help, you will win.

Remember, if He calls you, He will equip you. You have nothing to fear in His army.

I'll go where You send me, Jesus. Give me the supernatural courage and the skills I will need to do the work. Amen.

JESUS WANTS US TO BELIEVE WHEN WE CAN'T SEE

Then Jesus told him, "Because you have seen me, you have believed; blessed are those who have not seen and yet have believed."

JOHN 20:29 NIV

It's so easy to believe what you can see with your eyes. You witness a friend holding her newborn, and you hear the little one cry. Because you've seen and heard—two different senses coming into play—you believe that's a baby.

But what if you were told that someone you loved was expecting a baby in eight months. You couldn't see the child. You couldn't hear the child. He or she was safely enclosed in Mommy's womb. You would simply have to trust that mother and take her at her word.

That's what it's like to put your trust in Jesus. Even when you can't see, the baby's coming. Even when you can't hear, the little one is on the way.

Blind faith is exactly that. . .blind. When you can't see it yet, you believe it anyway.

Jesus wants you to believe even when you can't see.

Increase my faith, Lord. I want to believe even when I can't yet see it. Amen.

JESUS, A FASCINATING GOODBYE

*They were looking intently up into the sky as he was
going, when suddenly two men dressed in white stood
beside them. "Men of Galilee," they said, "why do you
stand here looking into the sky? This same Jesus, who
has been taken from you into heaven, will come back
in the same way you have seen him go into heaven."*

ACTS 1:10–11 NIV

Goodbyes are never easy. We say our farewells when the grown kids
go back to college or to their new homes. We kiss the grandkids
on their cheeks and cry a few tears after they leave. We hope and
pray life will be kind and that we'll see these loved ones again, but
we're also keenly aware of the fragility of life. Sometimes, we part
ways and never see that person again.

Jesus' disciples must have wondered, as they watched Jesus
rise into the clouds, if they would ever see Him again. And in the
years that followed, as they—one by one—gave their lives for the
gospel, they must have questioned, "Is it true?"

How remarkable to realize that all those great men of old are
seeing Him, even now, basking in the glory of heaven. Together.

---

*I will join them someday, Jesus! I'll spend
eternity with You. . .and with them! Amen.*

JESUS, THE CORNERSTONE

[Jesus is] "the stone you builders rejected,
which has become the cornerstone."

Acts 4:11 niv

Jesus called Himself the cornerstone. Have you ever pondered what that means? When a builder starts the masonry foundation of a new home, he sets the first stone into place. It becomes a reference point for every other stone that will go in. Basically, the position of the structure is entirely dependent on this cornerstone.

Now it makes more sense, right? Jesus is the first. All the other stones (humankind) take their place after Him. And the structure of our building, the tilt of the home, is entirely dependent on Him.

If you build your home on anything other than Jesus, you lose the structure. You can try, but, just as in the fable of the Three Little Pigs, the wolf can huff and puff and blow that house right down.

Build your life on Him. Your cornerstone will never fail you.

I'm building my life on You, my solid foundation, Jesus! Everything else in my life will line up as I place my trust in You. Amen.

JESUS, OUR SALVATION

Salvation is found in no one else, for there is no other name under heaven given to mankind by which we must be saved.

ACTS 4:12 NIV

There's no other name.

When you're trapped and feel there's no way out, you can call out every name in the book—your best friend, your spouse, your child, your boss. No one can truly save you except Jesus. Salvation is found in Him alone.

His is the only name under heaven that was given to mankind so that we could be saved not just from our rough circumstances but from death. He saved us for eternal life.

What do you need saving from today? Call on Jesus. At His name, every knee will bow and every tongue confess that He is Lord. That's one powerful name!

You are my salvation, Jesus. No one else can save me. Today, I call on You for help not just with the situations I find myself in but for my very life. Amen.

JESUS, FORGIVER OF SINS

Therefore, my friends, I want you to know that through Jesus the forgiveness of sins is proclaimed to you.

ACTS 13:38 NIV

Jesus' followers believed that He was who He said He was.

His opponents? They fought tooth and nail to bring Him down. They saw Him as a liar, a blasphemer, a divisive force come to interrupt their power play. In short, He was their enemy.

Perhaps the one claim that drove them crazy above all others was Jesus' words that He could forgive sin. These biblical intellectuals knew that this claim was also a claim of divinity. And that they could not allow.

Jesus not only claimed to forgive sins, He actually did forgive sins. He wasn't lying. He was—and is—one with the Father. He has the power to erase the sins of yesterday and give you a clean slate today.

Don't see Him as your enemy. See Him as your best friend, your great eraser, your salvation.

The old is gone. Behold, Jesus is making all things new.

I trust that You are who You claimed to be, Jesus. You are my salvation, the one who forgives my many sins! I put my trust in You. Amen.

JESUS DIED FOR THE WICKED

For when we were still helpless, Christ died for
the wicked at the time that God chose.
ROMANS 5:6 GNT

Have you ever done something so bad, so shocking, that you wondered if you could bounce back from it? Maybe you faced some sort of public humiliation and found yourself curled up in the corner, hiding away from the world. Nothing could save you from the embarrassing attention.

Then Jesus rushed in, brushed you off, spoke words of forgiveness, and put you on your feet again. Even in the midst of your messy state, He offered love, kindness, and hope.

That's the kind of Savior He is. Jesus comes when we're helpless and hopeless to remind us that He didn't die for saints. . .He died for sinners like you and me.

You're not alone, friend. You've done shameful things. We all have. That means you're exactly who He came for.

You died for me, Jesus. Thank You! Amen.

GRACE THROUGH JESUS CHRIST

*But the two are not the same, because God's free gift
is not like Adam's sin. It is true that many people died
because of the sin of that one man. But God's grace is
much greater, and so is his free gift to so many people
through the grace of the one man, Jesus Christ.*

ROMANS 5:15 GNT

Through one man (Adam), sin entered the world. Through one man (Jesus), grace and forgiveness overpowered sin. Funny, isn't it? The impact of one man.

Think back over the powerful people you've known in your life. If you had to choose one word to describe each of them and the impact they had on their family/community/workplace, what word would you choose? It might be hard to narrow it down to one word, but summarize each one's legacy in a word.

Now shift gears and think of yourself: What word will people choose to describe you after you're gone? Will they have trouble coming up with a succinct summary of your life, or have you made it easy for them?

For Adam, the word was *sin*. For Jesus, the word was *grace*.

For you? Well, that's totally up to you. Write that story while you can.

---

*Lord, I want to make an impact for You. I want to write
the right words on the hearts of those I love. Amen.*

IN UNION WITH JESUS

*For surely you know that when we were baptized into union
with Christ Jesus, we were baptized into union with his death.*

ROMANS 6:3 GNT

If you're married, you probably understand the concept of biblical union. When you marry someone, the two of you become one in God's sight, literally one flesh. When the Lord sees you, He sees your spouse. . .and vice versa.

That's how it is when you give your heart to Jesus too. You become one with Him. When people see you, they see Him. Your words of life are His words of life. Your smile is His smile. Your cup of cold water to one who's thirsty is His cup of water. Everything you do reflects Him.

So, how do you come into union with Him? You start by making Him Lord and Savior of your life. Give yourself to Him, and He will give Himself to you. Together, you will be a force for good in this world!

---

*I give myself to You afresh today, Jesus. I want to be
one with You. I am Yours and You are mine! Amen.*

HIS SPIRIT IN US

If the Spirit of God, who raised Jesus from death, lives in you, then he who raised Christ from death will also give life to your mortal bodies by the presence of his Spirit in you.

ROMANS 8:11 GNT

It's a great mystery, all of it: How the King of the universe can live in a heart. How the Spirit of God can dwell inside a human being. He's not just with us, He's in us. Mind boggling!

Here's an amazing promise from the Word of God: the same Spirit that raised Christ from the dead resides in us. This is a very specific promise. The Holy Spirit propelled Jesus from the grave. Now, He's living in you.

What does this mean? It means you have the same power inside of you, thanks to the Spirit of God. You have resurrection power, girl! So, stop fretting over things you can't control. The Holy Spirit is in charge now!

---

*I'm so glad you came to live inside of me.
You give me everything I need, Jesus. Amen.*

CONFESS JESUS TO RECEIVE LIFE

*If you confess that Jesus is Lord and believe that
God raised him from death, you will be saved.*

ROMANS 10:9 GNT

What you say matters. The words that come out of your mouth reflect two things—the thoughts in your head and the feelings in your heart. Words have power.

When you say, "I believe that Jesus is the Christ, the Son of the Living God" (Peter's confession), those words shake the stratosphere. If you truly believe them, they will change your life forever. They can change your family, your situation, your relationships.

The Bible makes a radical promise: if you make that confession, and if you believe it to be true, you will be saved. Picture a car going off a cliff, stopped just at the tipping point. You've been saved from the tipping point. Now, that's worth shouting over!

---

*Thank You for saving me, Jesus! I've been saved as I've put
my faith in You. Nothing will ever be the same. Amen.*

A BODY AT UNION WITH JESUS

*We have many parts in the one body, and all these parts
have different functions. In the same way, though we are
many, we are one body in union with Christ, and we are
all joined to each other as different parts of one body.*

ROMANS 12:4–5 GNT

Each part of your physical body plays a completely separate
role from the other. The mouth can't do what the hands can do.
The hands can't do what the feet can do. The feet can't do what
the brain can do. . .and so on. These "parts" are interdependent. They lean on each other.

That's how the body of Christ is when we walk in unity.
Some are hands. Some are feet. Some are mouthpieces. Some are
the brains of the operation. Take any one of those parts away, and
the whole body is handicapped.

You're meant to work together with fellow believers. They
might drive you crazy. They might not be like you in personality or technique, but they are your arms, feet, and eyes. Can you
really do without them? Would you want to?

---

*I get it, Jesus! Your body is beautifully woven together,
working as one. Help us to be unified. Amen.*

WE TAKE UP HIS WEAPONS

But take up the weapons of the Lord Jesus Christ, and stop
paying attention to your sinful nature and satisfying its desires.
ROMANS 13:14 GNT

What do you reach for when you're stressed? Chocolate? Potato
chips? The phone? The remote control?

Whatever you "take up" when you're overwhelmed says a lot
about you. Because we have a sinful nature, we often find ourselves
reaching for things that won't really make the situation better. In
fact, many of our solutions just exacerbate the problem.

God wants you to "take up" His weapons—the sword of the
Spirit, the shoes of peace, the helmet of salvation, and so on. If
this is your go-to (taking on the tools He's given you), then those
stressful situations you're facing will have better endings.

Today, I won't reach for the usual stuff, Jesus. Instead, I'll
turn to You. I'll implement the tools You've given me in
Your Word! I can win this battle with Your help! Amen.

JESUS ACCEPTS US

*Accept one another, then, for the glory of
God, as Christ has accepted you.*
ROMANS 15:7 GNT

Imagine someone gives you a gift. It's wrapped in lovely paper sitting on your kitchen table. You walk by it but don't open it. You don't utilize whatever is inside. It just sits there. You never accept it.

To accept something (or someone) means you take the time to unwrap the package and take a look at what's inside. Then you joyfully make use of it. You thank the giver for it. You see its value. It becomes a thing of beauty in your life.

That same principle applies when you accept a friend or loved one. You're saying to that person "I see value in you! I find you useful. I think you're a gift worth unwrapping! In fact, I'm going to thank the giver for sending you my way!"

See how beautiful life can be when you see each friend and family member this way?

---

*Jesus, thank You for sending so many, many people into
my life. They bring me joy. They have value. They are
worth my time and effort. I'm grateful for them. Amen.*

WE FELLOWSHIP WITH JESUS

God is to be trusted, the God who called you to have
fellowship with his Son Jesus Christ, our Lord.
1 Corinthians 1:9 gnt

To have fellowship with someone means you're in friendly association with him (or her). Think of it like this: you're "fellows" (friends) on the "ship" of life together. Might sound corny, but that's a pretty accurate description. When you're traveling in the same direction, united in strategy and outcome, the journey is a lot more fun.

Who are you in fellowship with today? What friend-ground have you surrounded yourself with? Make sure they're all in fellowship with Jesus so that you're all walking in unity. That way, you can grow in faith together. If you find yourself in a group that's pulling you away from fellowship with Jesus, it's time to make some new friends.

Thank You for guiding me to the right friends, Jesus. I
want to fellowship with them and with You. Show me
how to keep my relationships in balance so that I never
pull away from You, not even for a second. Amen.

FORGET EVERYTHING BUT JESUS

*For while I was with you, I made up my
mind to forget everything except Jesus Christ
and especially his death on the cross.*

1 CORINTHIANS 2:2 GNT

Maybe you've heard the phrase "Forget about it!" Saying that and doing it are two different things, however. It's not always easy to forget. When someone wounds you, for instance. Or when you're battling an enemy like cancer. Or when you're fired from your job for no good reason.

Some of the hardest things in life leave a lasting impression, one that's nearly impossible to forget. And yet God says, "Forget about it!" He wants you to focus your attention not on the "thing" that hurt you but on Him. When you're tempted to hyperfocus on the problem, shift your attention to Him. When you're convinced you can't climb out of the pit you're in, stop looking at the walls and look up.

Forget about it. No, really.

---

*I'll do my best to forget everything but You, Jesus.
I'm definitely going to need Your help with this one! Amen.*

ALL THINGS EXIST THROUGH JESUS

Yet for us there is one God, the Father, from whom are all things and for whom we exist, and one Lord, Jesus Christ, through whom are all things and through whom we exist.

1 Corinthians 8:6 esv

Imagine you have a lamp plugged into an outlet in your living room and another in your bedroom. In the kitchen, the overhead light has a bright bulb in it, and in the bathroom, the mirror is lit with several small bulbs.

All of those bulbs are attached to one power source. If you walk outside to the breaker box and flip the switch, you don't just lose the light in the bathroom. You lose it all. Everything runs in and through that breaker box.

The same is true with your relationship with Jesus. All things exist and are powered through Him. Remove Him from the equation, and nothing holds together. Relationships don't work. Talents get you nowhere. Job skills are pointless.

You exist for Him. Plug in today!

I'll stay plugged into You, Jesus. Nothing in my life makes sense when I pull away, so I'll stick close. Thank You for the power to accomplish all You've given me to do. Amen.

CHRIST. . .THE FULFILLMENT OF PROPHECY

*For I delivered to you as of first importance what I also
received: that Christ died for our sins in accordance with
the Scriptures, that he was buried, that he was raised
on the third day in accordance with the Scriptures.*

1 CORINTHIANS 15:3–4 ESV

Old Testament prophets shared all sorts of insights about the coming
Savior hundreds, if not thousands, of years before Jesus came on
the scene. If you really want to be impressed with God's continuity
line, study the prophetic timeline of Christ. It's remarkable, really.
The prophets said where He would be born, how He would be
received, even how He would be led as a lamb to the slaughter.
They got it right.

Once you see how accurate their predictions were, it's easier
to believe Jesus really was who He said He was. A fraud could
never have fulfilled all those prophecies. (Example: A normal baby
couldn't have arranged his own birthplace in Bethlehem.)

Jesus was—and is—the real deal. The prophecies are just the
icing on the cake in this remarkable God-story!

---

*I marvel at the details of Your life, Jesus! You truly
are who and what You claimed to be! Amen.*

RESURRECTION THROUGH JESUS

For since death came through a man, the resurrection
of the dead comes also through a man.

1 CORINTHIANS 15:21 NIV

We know that Jesus rose from the dead. We know that those who place their trust in Him will also be resurrected, raised to live in heaven with Him for eternity.

But did you realize that resurrection can happen here on earth too? It's true!

If you've ever been in the depths of despair (in a true depression) and risen from the ashes, you understand. You've been resurrected.

If you've ever found yourself buried deep in a sea of grief only to rise to the surface again, you get it. You've been resurrected.

If you've ever leaped from the bonds of an abusive relationship to be set free once more, you see the truth. You've been resurrected.

God is still in the resurrection business. No matter what you're going through today, He's big enough and strong enough to lift you out of it. Cry out to Him today.

I need resurrection in so many areas of my life, Jesus!
Thank You for caring enough to rescue me. Amen.

VICTORY IN JESUS

But thanks be to God, who gives us the
victory through our Lord Jesus Christ.
1 Corinthians 15:57 esv

There's only one way to win a battle. You have to take hold of God's hand and trust Him through the process.

Ask David, the shepherd boy. He faced the mighty giant Goliath. With a simple slingshot and a smooth stone, David took him down. But it wasn't really the stone that did Goliath in. It was God intervening on David's behalf. Let's face it: a little stone wouldn't have done the trick. But propelled from the hand of the Creator of the universe? That's a different matter altogether!

When you add God to the equation, when You place Him in charge of the battle you're facing, you'll always come out victorious. You won't have to wonder. You'll trust that He's going to give you the victory, even when the circumstances seem to say otherwise.

Trust Him in the battle. Victory is coming.

I won't take my eyes off You, Jesus. I'll include You in the battle. Take the slingshot from my hand and aim it with precision, I pray. Let's take the enemy down! Amen.

WE SHARE IN THE SUFFERINGS OF JESUS

For as we share abundantly in Christ's sufferings,
so through Christ we share abundantly in comfort too.
2 CORINTHIANS 1:5 ESV

Anyone who thinks that life is all sunshine, lollipops, and roses is woefully misguided. If you follow after Christ, you don't just share in His joys, you share in His sorrows. This is to be expected.

The same Jesus who was celebrated on the day of the triumphal entry is the same Savior who sweat drops of blood in the garden. He had glorious days and days when He was tormented and beaten by those who falsely accused Him. Jesus faced it all—the good, the bad, and the ugly.

You'll face it all too. There will be days when you weep and days when you rejoice. Just know that no matter what you're facing, He's been there too.

I'm so glad You've walked this road ahead of me, Jesus. Thank You for showing me the way on good days and bad. Amen.

A NEW CREATION IN JESUS

Therefore, if anyone is in Christ, he is a new creation.
The old has passed away; behold, the new has come.
2 CORINTHIANS 5:17 ESV

The old has passed away. Maybe you read that and say, "Yeah, right. I wish!" Perhaps you're dealing with some fallout from something you did yesterday. Or the day before. Or the year before.

When Jesus forgave your sins, He washed them away like water under a bridge. This means you don't have to allow the guilt or shame to consume you. Sure, you might have to work your way through some details, make some things right, but you're on a fresh path now.

Christ has made you a new creation. You're a butterfly emerging from the chrysalis. You're forgiven for the sins of yesterday.

You can live as one who has been set free.

Thank You for making me a new creation, Lord! I don't have to beat myself up anymore. Yesterday is gone. Today is brand new! Thank You for fresh opportunities. Amen.

GOD RECONCILED THE WORLD THROUGH JESUS

In Christ God was reconciling the world to himself,
not counting their trespasses against them, and
entrusting to us the message of reconciliation.

2 CORINTHIANS 5:19 ESV

To "reconcile" means to reestablish a close relationship with someone.

During Old Testament times, the world pulled away from God. They broke His laws and broke His heart. Then He sent His Son and re-established relationship with mankind. If not for Jesus, the chasm between mankind and God would remain. But because of Jesus, we have access into the throne room.

Now that we've been reconciled, God sees us as pure. We are washed clean. We don't have to worry that He won't want anything to do with us. We're reconciled. He's dying to spend time with us. . .literally.

Thank You for reconciling us, Jesus! If not for You, I wouldn't have access to my heavenly Father. I'm so grateful that You saved the world so that we could be in relationship. Amen.

HIS POWER IS PERFECT IN WEAKNESS

But he said to me, "My grace is sufficient for you, for
my power is made perfect in weakness." Therefore
I will boast all the more gladly of my weaknesses,
so that the power of Christ may rest upon me.
2 CORINTHIANS 12:9 ESV

Have you ever heard the expression "When I'm weak, He's strong"?
It's so true! When you are at your very weakest, the strength of
your Savior shines through.

Here's the problem. People always say, "Just be strong!" But
there are times when you simply can't. Instead of pretending to be
strong when you're not, maybe it would be better to admit your
weakness and lean on Him. Jesus won't let you down. His power
is perfected in your weakness.

"Therefore I will boast of my weaknesses." Can you say that
yet? It might take some time, but when you develop a "He's strong,
I don't have to be" mentality, you'll be freed. It's not up to you. It
never was.

I'm so weak at times, Lord, and I'm tired of pretending
to be strong when I'm really falling apart inside. Thank
You for being strong when I'm weak. Amen.

WE ARE ALL ONE IN JESUS

There is neither Jew nor Greek, there is neither slave nor free, there is no male and female, for you are all one in Christ Jesus.

GALATIANS 3:28 ESV

We live in a very divisive time in history. People raise their fists at one another based on all sorts of differences. Politics. Race. Religion. You name it, the world is fighting about it.

How wonderful to walk into a church and see all the believers—in every color, every ethnicity—worshipping alongside one another. It's a beautiful sight, isn't it?

God intends for His body to be "one" in Him. We're not supposed to separate ourselves by culture. Or race. Or whether we're male or female. We're not supposed to divide ourselves into factions—all the rich folks in this group and all the poor ones in that one.

The goal of our walk with Christ is to love Him and love people. When we truly do that, we can become the body He intended.

Make me one with those around me, Lord. Help me put aside my differences and love as You love. Amen.

DON'T BE CHAINED AGAIN

Christ made us free. Stay that way. Do not get chained all over again in the Law and its kind of religious worship.
GALATIANS 5:1 NLV

Imagine you were in prison for a crime you didn't commit. Finally, the day came for your release. The judge heard your plea, and your sentence was reversed. You walked free, out into the sunshine, for the first time in ages.

How would it feel to finally be set free? The very last thing you would want would be a trip back to the cell that held you. Freedom is too precious!

That's how it is when you come to Christ. He sets you free from the chains that held you. It might be tempting to go back to your old lifestyle, but remember that feeling of being in prison? It's not worth it. Sin, no matter how "fun" in the moment, always leads to bondage. You've been there. Done that. Don't go back.

I've been set free, Jesus. Thank You for loosening my chains and letting me walk free from the prison that once held me! Amen.

REBORN IN CHRIST!

But God had so much loving-kindness. He loved us with such a great love. Even when we were dead because of our sins, He made us alive by what Christ did for us. You have been saved from the punishment of sin by His loving-favor.
EPHESIANS 2:4–5 NLV

If you've ever been through a season of drought, you know how hard it can be on your lawn. Instead of being lush and green, brown patches appear. Before long, the whole yard is crispy and beyond repair. You water as you're able, but it's too little to save the situation.

Sometimes, when you think there's no hope for the lawn, tiny blades of grass will peek through, surprising you. Underneath the surface of death, life emerges, offering hope.

That's how it is when you give your heart to Jesus. No matter how cracked or dry the surface, no matter how caked or hard your heart might be, He can make it spring to life again. That's how much your heavenly Father loves you.

Thank You for new life, Jesus! Even at my worst, You breathed life and changed everything. How grateful I am! Amen.

WE WORK FOR JESUS

We are His work. He has made us to belong to Christ Jesus so we can work for Him. He planned that we should do this.
EPHESIANS 2:10 NLV

Whom do you work for? Who's the driving force behind why you do all you do?

Some people would say, "I work for the boss-man. I do whatever he tells me."

Others would say, "I work to pay the light bill and the mortgage." Some would add, "I work to put a roof over my kids' heads."

Those are all legitimate responses, but they don't really answer the real question. Whom do you work for?

Today's verse from Ephesians makes it plain that we belong to Jesus, and we were created and designed to work for Him. It was all planned in advance. So every task you fulfill, every toilet you scrub. . .it's all for Him.

That's a nice change of perspective, isn't it? Work for Him, and be blessed in all you do.

I get it, Jesus. I'm not working to pay the bills. I'm not working to make my boss happy. I'm Your child, created to work for You. Amen.

BROUGHT CLOSE TO JESUS

But now you belong to Christ Jesus. At one time you were far away from God. Now you have been brought close to Him. Christ did this for you when He gave His blood on the cross.
EPHESIANS 2:13 NLV

When you adopt a shelter dog, the getting-to-know-you process can be tedious. Some dogs aren't comfortable around people, especially if they have experienced abuse in the past. They pull away and recoil at your touch.

It takes weeks—sometimes months—of working with these wounded animals to get them to come around, but you'll never be sorry for the effort you put in. When they finally curl up in your lap or rest their head on your knee, your heart will melt.

Isn't that how God must feel when we finally relinquish and give our hearts and our trust fully to Him? Once we relax in His tender loving care, once we realize we are safe with Him, everything changes.

Drawing close is easy when you're at home with the one you love.

Draw me close, Jesus. I'm most at home when I'm with You. Amen.

GROW UP AND BE LIKE JESUS

Instead, speaking the truth in love, we will grow to become in every respect the mature body of him who is the head, that is, Christ.

EPHESIANS 4:15 NIV

"Grow up, why don't you?" Maybe you've used these words with your kids (or your spouse). That brusque, inflammatory question is really more of an accusation than anything else. It's our way of saying, "Stop acting like a child!"

Here's the thing, though. We all act like children at times. We all get stubborn and rebellious. And we could just as easily look at the reflection in the mirror and say, "Grow up!" to ourselves on any given day.

Jesus wants us to grow up. He longs for us to be more like Him. We are to put away childish things—like temper tantrums, rebellion, and our me-first attitude—and focus on Him and on the work to be done.

What areas of your life need work today? Maybe it's time to grow up, girl!

I get it, Jesus. I'm still clinging to some childish behaviors. Show me what needs to go, then help me rid myself of these things. Amen.

JESUS, A GIFT ON THE ALTAR

*Live with love as Christ loved you. He gave Himself for us,
a gift on the altar to God which was as a sweet smell to God.*
EPHESIANS 5:2 NLV

Have you ever given someone a gift—say, a gift card—only to have them turn around and use it for you? Some people are so generous, aren't they?

This is just how God treats that gift you've given Him.

In Old Testament times, the high priest would offer a sacrifice to God on an altar. The altar was a special, holy place, set aside for these special offerings.

Your heart is an altar. It's a holy place where you offer things to Jesus. What sort of things? Your attitude. Your word choices. Your temperament. Your will. Your actions. Your desires.

If you're willing to lay all those things on the altar, He will take them and breathe life into them. He will take your gift, your offering, and use it for your good.

My heart is an altar, Jesus. Thank You for meeting me there. Amen.

CHRIST, THE HEAD OF THE CHURCH

Wives, obey your own husbands. In doing this, you obey the Lord. For a husband is the head of his wife as Christ is the head of the church. It is His body (the church) that He saves.

Ephesians 5:22–23 nlv

Have you ever heard someone say, "She's the brains of the operation"? What they're really saying is "She's the driving force, the one with the vision."

God is the brains of the operation. He's in control of it all, including every aspect of your life. If you try to remove Him from the equation, the operation fails. There's no easy way to say it. Take Him out, and it all craters.

Christ is the head of the church. In these crazy times we live in, it's important to remember that we have to keep Him front and center. His Word. His will. His heart for mankind. This isn't the time to soften His message or pull away from His Word. This is the time to draw closer than ever. If we ever needed "the brains of the operation," it's now.

Jesus, we're counting on You. We'll stick close to Your Word, Your plan, Your vision. May we never stray from the only one who truly sees what's ahead. Amen.

GOD WILL COMPLETE THE GOOD WORK IN US

I am sure that God Who began the good work in you will keep on working in you until the day Jesus Christ comes again.

PHILIPPIANS 1:6 NLV

God finishes what He starts. He's not like us in that regard. We start things and then give up when we get bored or when we're weary. He never gets bored. He never gets weary.

This is a wonderful promise, isn't it? Today, if you're worried about a wayward child or a problem that seems to have no resolution, remember that God finishes what He starts. Every time. He who began a good work in you—or your loved one—will be faithful to complete it, no matter what the circumstances look like at this very moment.

You're going to finish it, God. You always finish well. I can trust You in my life and in the lives of my loved ones. What a trustworthy God You are! Amen.

TO LIVE IS CHRIST

*To me, living means having Christ. To die
means that I would have more of Him.*

PHILIPPIANS 1:21 NLV

There is no life outside of Christ. He's the oxygen you need to survive, the very air in your lungs. Many people throughout the ages have tried to live without Him. Many are still trying. But they are simply moving through life, not genuinely experiencing the depth of what He intends it to be.

Life in Christ is exciting. It's supernatural. It's faith-filled. Life in Christ is vibrant and alive, ever changing as you grow in Him. And it's filled with possibilities.

And here's the best part of all—even after this life ends, your life in Christ goes on and on. To die means you have even more of Him. The bliss of heaven will far supersede even the best day on earth.

I'm so glad to be alive in You, Jesus! To live with You and to spend eternity with You? Even better! Thank You for giving me life. Amen.

THINK LIKE JESUS

Think as Christ Jesus thought.
PHILIPPIANS 2:5 NLV

Have you ever heard the phrase "You need to get rid of your stinkin' thinkin'"? Some people really struggle with their thought life. No matter what the circumstances might be, they find themselves wrestling, wrestling, wrestling with how to interpret it.

Maybe you're one of those "overthinkers." Maybe you overanalyze absolutely everything. Or maybe you're impulsive and barely think things through before jumping into something. Both of those approaches have their downfalls.

Here's the thing: You can think like Christ. You can have the mind of Christ. You can approach every circumstance, every situation, with the "What would Jesus do?" mind-set.

It's more than a cliché. Thinking like Him is key.

What would You do in this current situation I'm walking through, Jesus? I want to respond as You would respond, so give me Your thoughts over the situation. Amen.

JESUS BECAME A SERVANT

Jesus has always been as God is. But He did not hold to His rights as God. He put aside everything that belonged to Him and made Himself the same as a servant who is owned by someone. He became human by being born as a man. After He became a man, He gave up His important place and obeyed by dying on a cross.
PHILIPPIANS 2:6–8 NLV

Pride is a funny thing, isn't it? We always want to be acknowledged for what we do, who we are, our many talents and abilities. We hate to be overlooked.

Isn't it ironic that Jesus, the most creative one of all, didn't care one whit about any of that? When He became human, he gave up His desire for notoriety. As this verse says, "He gave up His important place."

There was no pride involved in Jesus' walk here on earth. No squared shoulders. No puffed-up attitude. None of the things we would deal with. He laid it all down out of His great love for mankind.

Show me how to lay down my pride so I can be more like You, Jesus. I don't want to be puffed up. May my pride not be an "important place" to me. Amen.

JESUS, ABOVE EVERYTHING ELSE

Because of this, God lifted Jesus high above everything else.
He gave Him a name that is greater than any other name. So
when the name of Jesus is spoken, everyone in heaven and
on earth and under the earth will bow down before Him.
PHILIPPIANS 2:9–10 NLV

If someone asked you for a list of "big names," what names would you add to the list? Politicians? Singers? Actors or actresses?

Maybe you would skip all of that and add the names of people who've made a direct impact in your life—parents, siblings, spouse, friends, church leaders.

But no matter how great any of those people are, Jesus is above all. His name is higher than the president's. His love is greater than even the most loving mother. His provision is greater than even the most capable father.

Jesus is the name above every name, and when you speak that name, everything in heaven and on earth comes to a screeching halt, bowing in reverence.

What an amazing name. . .Jesus!

Yours is the name above all names,
Jesus. May I never forget. Amen.

THE POWER THAT RAISED JESUS FROM THE DEAD

I want to know Him. I want to have the same power in my life that raised Jesus from the dead. I want to understand and have a share in His sufferings and be like Christ in His death.

Philippians 3:10 nlv

Can you even imagine the power that was available to Jesus to come out of that grave? Talk about miraculous! We're talking resurrection power here—the kind that breathes life into impossible situations.

That same power lives in you. Resurrection power is yours for the taking. When you're a blood-bought child of the King, He gives you the power for radical transformation. He gives you the miraculous.

What areas of your life are wilted right now? Which ones have been buried in graveclothes? Instead of giving up, give it over to Jesus. Ask for His resurrection power to breathe life into the situation, into the person, into the problem. He can, in one breath, bring things to life once again.

There are things in my life that are buried deep, Jesus. They seem lifeless and cold. I can't imagine them resurrecting, springing to life. But You can! Today, I ask for Your resurrection power over my life, my circumstances, and my relationships. Amen.

KEEP YOUR EYE ON THE CROWN

My eyes are on the crown. I want to win the race and get the crown of God's call from heaven through Christ Jesus.

PHILIPPIANS 3:14 NLV

When an athlete competes, he's usually got his eye on the prize. He wants that Olympic gold medal. Nothing else will do.

When you run the race for Jesus, there's a prize, for sure. But it's not a gold medal. It's not a moment on a stage with the eyes of the nation—or the globe—on you. You won't hear your national anthem; you won't smile and wave as people applaud your greatness. There will be none of that.

When you compete, your eye is on the crown. Eternity. Life forever with Him. Knowing you'll one day spend eternity in His presence makes all the speedbumps in life's race seem insignificant.

Keep running the race. There's a very big prize coming, girl.

I'll keep going even when I don't feel like it, Jesus. The prize is eternity with You. How could I stop now? Amen.

CITIZENS OF HEAVEN

But we are citizens of heaven, where the Lord Jesus Christ lives.
And we are eagerly waiting for him to return as our Savior.
PHILIPPIANS 3:20 NLT

If you want to travel to a foreign country, you acquire a passport. That passport opens the door to other nations. You'll always be a citizen of your own country, but you have the freedom to travel with passport in hand.

In much the same way, you are a permanent citizen of heaven. From the moment you put your trust in Jesus, that passport is handed to you. But while you're here on earth, you're free to travel—to do and be all God has called you to do and be.

No matter where you go, no matter what you do, always remember that your true citizenship is in heaven not here on earth. Don't get too caught up in earthly things. One day all these things you're struggling with will fade to nothing. Your citizenship in heaven will be all that remains.

I'm so glad my citizenship is with You, Jesus! Amen.

HIS GLORIOUS RICHES

*And this same God who takes care of me will
supply all your needs from his glorious riches,
which have been given to us in Christ Jesus.*

PHILIPPIANS 4:19 NLT

If someone said, "Make a wish list of everything you want," what would go on the list? No doubt you have a lot of wishes and wants.

Of course, there's a difference between a want and a need. God doesn't promise to supply all your wants, but He absolutely assures you that He will supply all your needs. This is a promise that came through your relationship with Jesus Christ, His precious Son. God never let His Son down, and He will never let you down either. His glorious riches are available to you. God owns the cattle on a thousand hills. If He cares for the fish of the sea and the birds of the air, He will certainly give you all you need.

---

*You take care of me from Your vast supply, Jesus. You have
untapped riches, and You're able to meet my needs, no matter
how great. I will put my trust in You, my provider. Amen.*

THE KINGDOM OF JESUS

*For he has rescued us from the kingdom of darkness
and transferred us into the Kingdom of his dear Son,
who purchased our freedom and forgave our sins.*

COLOSSIANS 1:13–14 NLT

If you've ever been rescued from a life-threatening situation such as an abusive relationship, you know the freedom of stepping out into the light after being in the dark for so long. At first, you can hardly believe it. Are you really safe? Is this real? Is there hope for a better future ahead?

That's how it is when you give your heart to Christ. He rescues you from the kingdom of darkness. He immediately transfers you to the sunlight. In that moment, the grace and peace of your Savior wash over you, making all things new. You're placed on the kingdom road, one bought and paid for by Jesus Christ on the cross.

You're rescued. Transferred. Born again. You're a child of the kingdom now. Don't ever forget it!

---

*I'm a daughter of the Most High God, already walking
kingdom's road. Thank You for my freedom, Jesus! Amen.*

CHRIST LIVES IN US

For God wanted them to know that the riches and glory of Christ are for you Gentiles, too. And this is the secret: Christ lives in you. This gives you assurance of sharing his glory.

COLOSSIANS 1:27 NLT

"Shh! Lean in close! Want to hear a secret?"

What happens when you hear those words? You take them seriously, right? You want to be in the know, in the inner loop. You want to be privy to top-secret information.

God shared a lot of top-secret info in His Word. One of the key messages is found in these simple words: "This is the secret: Christ lives in you."

How is that even possible, for someone to live inside of someone else? On the surface, it makes no sense. But the Spirit of God is living and breathing in every person who bows the knee to Christ. It's no longer you living. . .it's Him. In Him, you live and breathe and have fullness of life! All the riches and glory of Christ are yours for the taking now that He lives inside of you!

---

*I'm so grateful You came to live in my heart, Jesus!
You've given me access to all that You have and
all that You are. I'm so very grateful! Amen.*

JESUS: GOD'S MYSTERIOUS PLAN

I want them to be encouraged and knit together by strong ties
of love. I want them to have complete confidence that they
understand God's mysterious plan, which is Christ himself.

COLOSSIANS 2:2 NLT

Have you ever heard anyone say, "Just work the plan and the plan will work"? Oftentimes, that is the case. If you just stick with the program, you'll usually get to a solid ending.

Jesus was God's mysterious plan. There was no Plan B. If Jesus changed His mind and decided not to go through with the walk to Calvary, where would we be today? It's hard to say.

Jesus worked the plan and the plan worked. And He wants you to stick with His plan too. When He places you on a road and gives you marching orders, it's not good to give up a few steps in. You need to keep going, even when the plan is a little too mysterious for your liking.

Be encouraged. Have complete confidence. Soon enough, you will fully understand the plan.

I'm sticking with You, Jesus. I might not comprehend
everything now, but I trust You implicitly. Thank
You for creating a plan for my life. Amen.

CHRIST, RULER AND AUTHORITY

For in Christ lives all the fullness of God in a human body. So you also are complete through your union with Christ, who is the head over every ruler and authority.

Colossians 2:9–10 nlt

Jesus Christ was the fullness of God in a human body. If you've seen Jesus, you've seen the Father. The same thing can be said of you now that you've given your heart to Christ. See _____ (insert your name), you've seen the Father.

You're a direct reflection of the Lord. He dwells inside of you. And the world is watching. There's no doubt about that. It's important to do your best to represent Team Jesus well—in your actions, the way you speak to others, and especially how you treat those inside your own home. Let's face it, that's often the hardest one of all.

You don't have to do this alone. Christ, who lives inside of you, is the ultimate ruler and authority over all things. Lean on Him, and you'll naturally be more like Him.

I want to be like You, Jesus. Today, I lean on You—the one who is the fullness of God in human form! May I represent You well! Amen.

THE PEACE OF CHRIST

And let the peace that comes from Christ rule in
your hearts. For as members of one body you are
called to live in peace. And always be thankful.
COLOSSIANS 3:15 NLT

Imagine a country with no ruler. No king. No queen. No president. No congress. No governors. No court system.

Some people (especially those who are fed up with politics) might look at that and say, "Sounds good to me!" These things always sound good until anarchy breaks out.

The same is true with your heart. If you don't allow God to rule and reign over it, eventually there's going to be anarchy. You need a governor over your emotions. You need to hold court with the King to make sure your thoughts align with His. You need to make Him Lord of all of that, which means you must hand over the reins. Giving God complete control will end in the best possible outcome because He loves you intensely—so much that He sent His Son, whose very heart broke for you.

Thank You for the peace that rules my
heart as I give it to You, Jesus!

WHEN JESUS RETURNS

For since we believe that Jesus died and was raised to
life again, we also believe that when Jesus returns, God
will bring back with him the believers who have died.
1 THESSALONIANS 4:14 NLT

It's not a matter of "if" Jesus returns, it's a matter of when. He promised that He would come back, and we await His return with great joy and anticipation.

The world is in chaos. Things are kind of a hot mess right now. No matter where you stand on the political spectrum, you have to admit that people have turned against each other, sometimes even in their own families, and the quarreling is out of control.

Heaven is starting to look really good. And Jesus will come back for His bride to take her home. We don't know when. We don't know the particulars that will entail. But we can rest assured He's still very interested in what we're going through and will one day sweep us home.

I want to be ready for that day, Jesus. Prepare my heart. May I be
ready for eternity with You, no matter when that day comes. Amen.

JESUS, EVER PATIENT

But God had mercy on me so that Christ Jesus could use me as a prime example of his great patience with even the worst sinners. Then others will realize that they, too, can believe in him and receive eternal life.

1 TIMOTHY 1:16 NLT

Maybe you've heard the expression "She has the patience of Job." Job was a man who lived in Old Testament times who went through terrible trials. When someone compares you to Job, they're really admiring your patience level!

Take a look at today's verse. God wants your patience level to be compared to someone else's. Be like Jesus. Be a great example of what it's like to have to live among sinners without losing your cool.

When a conversation in heaven ensues about you, let it be "Hey, check out this one! She's a prime example, holding on for dear life!"

Holding on is far better than letting go. So, wrap your proverbial fingers around His hand today and become an example that will change those around you.

I want to be a good example, Lord! Help me, I pray. Amen.

JESUS, OUR MEDIATOR

There is one God and one Mediator who can reconcile God and humanity—the man Christ Jesus.
1 TIMOTHY 2:5 NLT

If you ever found yourself in jail after being falsely accused, you would need an attorney—preferably the best one out there! Only a good attorney can get you out of a jam like that!

Even when you're guilty, a mediator is key. He (or she) stands between you and the judge or jury. He takes the heat. He has the strategy. He puts himself on the line for you.

Jesus is the best mediator out there. He literally laid it all on the line when He went to the cross for you. He looked at the jury box, where the enemy sat with all of his henchmen, and said, "This one is innocent. She's covered by My blood. Case closed!"

It remains closed too! He truly covered it all. Don't let the enemy convince you otherwise. He already lost this case more than two thousand years ago.

Thank You for serving as my mediator, Jesus. I have nothing to fear as long as You are representing me. The enemy is defeated, thanks to You! I'm set free! Amen.

THERE IS STRENGTH IN HIS GRACE

You then, my son, be strong in the grace that is in Christ Jesus.
2 TIMOTHY 2:1 NIV

When you think about being strong, maybe your thoughts shift to the gym. Lifting weights. Working out. Getting fit. Building muscles.

Those things are all well and good, but there's a completely different way to get fit. God wants you to be strong in grace.

You might read that and think, *Wait. Grace? What does that have to do with strength? Aren't "grace-filled" people considered more softhearted?*

Sometimes it takes more strength to offer grace to someone when they've lashed out at you or hurt you in some way. It takes significant internal strength not to fight back when they come out swinging against you.

Grace takes strength. But no worries! You have plenty of it now that you're walking with Jesus!

I'm filled with Your grace, Jesus, which is why I know I must be strong! You've been so gracious to me. Help me to extend that same grace to others. Amen.

FOLLOWING JESUS ISN'T AN EASY ROAD

In fact, everyone who wants to live a godly
life in Christ Jesus will be persecuted.
2 TIMOTHY 3:12 NIV

Imagine you're on a road trip. There's a superhighway that will get you to your destination in an hour's time. There's a side road—paved in gravel and dirt—that will take three hours. Which one will you take?

Many people deliberately exit the off-ramp from their spiritual life and get on the bumpy road. They're attracted by temptation, thinking that road will actually bring more pleasure. Then they start hitting potholes and dead ends and miles and miles of desolation, away from safety.

At that point, they get it. They should've stuck to the superhighway!

Today, stay on the highway. Don't leave Jesus. Don't be tempted by things that look bright, shiny, easy, or exciting. His way is the best way. He won't let you down. And girl, you will arrive in style if you stick with Him!

I'll stick with You on the superhighway, Jesus. I won't
be swayed by things that tempt me. Amen.

BETTER PROMISES

But in fact the ministry Jesus has received is as superior to theirs as the covenant of which he is mediator is superior to the old one, since the new covenant is established on better promises.

Hebrews 8:6 niv

The covenant of Jesus was established on "better promises." What does that mean, exactly?

In Old Testament times, people were expected to follow the letter of the Law. Their salvation depended on their own actions. They simply weren't capable, which is why the High Priest had to enter the Holy of Holies once a year and offer a sacrifice on behalf of the people.

When Jesus came, His blood was more perfect than that of a spotless lamb. He was the ultimate sacrifice, the only one whose blood could cleanse for all eternity. His blood makes a better way. His blood is the better promise. And His blood is the only guarantee you will ever have that you can spend eternity with Him.

Thank You, Jesus, for being the better promise! You did what the Law could not. You cleansed and purged us not just for a brief time but for all eternity! I'm so grateful for the covenant I have with You. Amen.

A CLEANSED CONSCIENCE

How much more, then, will the blood of Christ, who through the eternal Spirit offered himself unblemished to God, cleanse our consciences from acts that lead to death, so that we may serve the living God!
HEBREWS 9:14 NIV

Imagine your car is filthy. You've been driving on a dirt road in the rain, and it's caked in mud. Where do you take it for a scrub—the local car wash known for its deep-cleaning or the ten-year-old next door who's raising money for summer camp?

When you have a big problem, you need a big solution. There will be other times to support the boy next door. Right now you need someone who can do a thorough job.

Jesus saw the mess that you used to be before you knew Him. You were caked in spiritual mud, and it didn't want to come off you. Your big problem required a big solution, so He cleansed you in the most remarkable way—by offering Himself as a sacrifice for you on the cross.

You are clean. . .indeed! Inside and out. He purged that icky, sticky mess—your yesterday—off you. Now you can stand before Him with a clean conscience, knowing His work is complete.

Thank You for cleansing me, Jesus. Only Your blood was powerful enough for a problem as big as mine. Amen.

JESUS RAN WITH PERSEVERANCE

Therefore, since we are surrounded by such a great cloud
of witnesses, let us throw off everything that hinders
and the sin that so easily entangles. And let us run with
perseverance the race marked out for us, fixing our eyes
on Jesus, the pioneer and perfecter of faith. For the joy
set before him he endured the cross, scorning its shame,
and sat down at the right hand of the throne of God.
HEBREWS 12:1–2 NIV

Have you ever trained for a marathon? Running a long race is a lot different from running a short one. During a shorter race, you take off at the fastest possible clip and keep up the pace until you hit your goal. With a longer race, you pace yourself. Why? So that you don't overexert initially and give up at the halfway point.

Running the race with Jesus is a lot like that. You have to pace yourself. Slow things down long enough to spend time with Him. That way you can persevere all the way to the end.

Don't give up! Catch a breath and keep going!

I'll pace myself, Jesus. I won't get out ahead of You. Amen.

JESUS NEVER CHANGES

Jesus Christ is the same yesterday and today and forever.
HEBREWS 13:8 NIV

If you pulled out all your school pictures and set them side by side in order by year, you would easily see the progression of your aging process. Kindergarten, soft curls and a playful smile. First grade, toothless. Second grade, crooked bangs. Sixth grade, looking a little awkward. Eighth grade, a few pimples. Graduation from high school, a young adult, ready to take on the world.

Of course, it's the same you in every photo. But the external you changes routinely.

Now think about Jesus. The Bible says He's the same yesterday, today, and forever. His picture isn't changing. His Word isn't changing. His promises aren't changing. His love isn't changing. You'll never have to wonder about your consistent, unmovable God! He's as crazy about you now as ever.

I'm so grateful You haven't changed, Jesus. I can still put my trust in You, my unshakable, unchanging God! Amen.

KEEP YOUR MIND READY FOR ACTION

*So then, have your minds ready for action. Keep alert
and set your hope completely on the blessing which
will be given you when Jesus Christ is revealed.*

1 PETER 1:13 GNT

Have you ever disengaged from a conversation? Maybe you were
with someone who droned on and on and you checked out. You
started thinking about something else altogether. You couldn't seem
to help yourself. Paying attention was impossible.

When it comes to following Jesus, staying engaged is critical.
He's always speaking, but are you always listening? No doubt
there are times when you tune out His voice. Or maybe the other
voices—friends, job, kids, church—get in the way. You can hear
Him off in the distance, but staying focused is hard.

Today, tune in. Listen hard. Do your best to drown out the
other voices. His is the one that matters most.

---

*Jesus, I'm listening! I don't want to be distracted by
other voices. I'll pay attention to You. Amen.*

THE COSTLY SACRIFICE OF CHRIST

*For you know what was paid to set you free from
the worthless manner of life handed down by your
ancestors. It was not something that can be destroyed,
such as silver or gold; it was the costly sacrifice of
Christ, who was like a lamb without defect or flaw.*

1 PETER 1:18–19 GNT

Imagine you had a family heirloom, one passed down through the generations. You guarded it with your life, knowing the value. No one could wrestle it from your hands. (Hey, when you understand the value of a thing, you go out of your way to make sure it's well guarded.)

The sacrifice of Christ on the cross is the most valuable gift you will ever receive. It's more priceless than any heirloom. Cherish it. Treat it with the care it deserves. This is one gift that can't be lost, can't be stolen, and can't be destroyed. Jesus gave it willingly, though it cost Him everything.

What a costly sacrifice. What an unfathomable gift.

---

*Jesus, thank You for the gift of salvation. What a price
You paid! I can never repay You, but I will spend my life
sharing the news of what You've done for me! Amen.*

A REVERENCE FOR JESUS IN YOUR HEART

But have reverence for Christ in your hearts, and honor
him as Lord. Be ready at all times to answer anyone
who asks you to explain the hope you have in you.

1 PETER 3:15 GNT

When you have reverence for someone, it means you have a deep respect for them. God wants you to have a reverence for Jesus in your heart. This means you don't take Him—or His name—lightly. When you think of Jesus, you're immediately in awe.

Your words bring Him honor. Your actions bring Him honor. And because you revere Him, people will notice. They will say, "This Christianity thing. . .you make it seem real."

Because it is real. And it has changed you for all eternity.

Jesus, I stand in awe of You. The hope inside of
my heart is all because of You. May it show to
everyone I come in contact with. Amen.

KEEP THE MESSAGE OF JESUS IN YOUR HEART

Be sure, then, to keep in your hearts the message you heard from the beginning. If you keep that message, then you will always live in union with the Son and the Father.

1 JOHN 2:24 GNT

Have you ever had an amazing conversation with a friend, then walked away and forgotten how deep, how personal, and how touching it was? We humans have a very short attention span sometimes, don't we?

When it comes to our relationship with Jesus, we need to have a long attention span. We should never forget all He's done for us. Keep the message of Jesus in your heart so that it spills out at the drop of a hat. When you need it, you won't have to go looking for it.

Here's one thing that will help: the message never changes. Jesus is the same yesterday, today, and forever and so is His message for mankind. He loves us. And that, dear woman of God, never changes.

I will keep Your message front and center in my heart, Jesus! May I never forget Your deep, abiding love. Amen.

WE GIVE OUR LIVES AS HE DID

*This is how we know what love is: Christ gave his life
for us. We too, then, ought to give our lives for others!*
1 JOHN 3:16 GNT

Jesus gave. And if we want to be like Him, we need to be givers too.

Give what, you ask?

Well, what do you have? A heart to love others? Money to assist with those in need? Time to help the ones who need help? Food to help the hungry? A cup of cold water to give to the thirsty?

There are a thousand different ways you can give of your time, talents, and treasures. Use your imagination. Take a look at the people around you and their particular needs. How can you help?

If you want to be like Jesus, take the time to figure out a "giving" plan. It might be simpler than you think.

---

*I want to be a giver like You, Jesus. You gave Your love,
Your healing touch, Your provision, and Your very life. May
I learn from Your example and give as You gave. Amen.*

WHY GOD SENT JESUS

*And God showed his love for us by sending his only Son
into the world, so that we might have life through him.*
1 John 4:9 GNT

God entered into covenant with the Israelites in Old Testament days. They did their best to live by the Law but kept getting off course. So God implemented a new covenant, one that included sending His Son to die for them, to save them once and for all.

The purpose of sending Jesus was to save the world. Not one particular people group. Not one ethnicity. Not one gender. Not one continent. Not one city or state.

Jesus came for us all. Every single person. And as many as would put their trust in Him. . .that's how many will be part of His kingdom.

He longs for all to know Him, which is why we must follow in His footsteps and get the message out. He didn't just come for us. He came for them.

---

*There are so many who still need to know You, Jesus! I know
You came not just for me but for the whole world. Help me
as I step out to share that message wherever I go. Amen.*

LIVING IN UNION WITH HIM

*If we declare that Jesus is the Son of God, we live in
union with God and God lives in union with us.*

1 JOHN 4:15 GNT

If you're "in union" with someone, you have a common interest or
purpose. Say you joined a local ministry that focused on feeding the
poor at homeless shelters. You would work together to accomplish
the task. You would be like-minded.

Jesus wants us to be in union with fellow believers. We should
have common goals, common strategies, and hearts filled with love
for each other and those we're trying to reach.

It's not always easy, though. There will be plenty of people
inside the walls of your own church who will be difficult to love.
They'll grate on your last nerve.

Put those feelings behind you and do the best you can to live
at peace in union with each other.

There's work to do! Link arms and get 'er done!

---

*Thank You for the reminder that I need to remain in union with my
fellow believers as much as I'm able. I'll do my best, Jesus. Amen.*

WE CAN DEFEAT THE WORLD

*Who can defeat the world? Only the person
who believes that Jesus is the Son of God.*

1 JOHN 5:5 GNT

Picture a prize fighter in the ring. He's tough. He's unbeatable...or so he thinks. Into the ring steps a little guy. Someone who's not accustomed to fighting. But he's been called by God to enter this battle, so there he is, ready to give it a try. He starts swinging, and to everyone's surprise, he catches the big guy off guard and knocks him to the ground.

When you feel like the little guy in the ring, boxing it out with the enemy of your soul, remember that God has called you to defeat the world. It's not a cliché to say that "with God all things are possible." Those words are 100 percent true when you enter the ring on His heels.

He will fight your battles for you. Only be still and wait for the right moment to take the enemy down.

---

*I won't let the enemy get me down, Jesus. With
Your help, I can defeat him. . .and the things of
this world. Keep me strong, I pray. Amen.*

YOUR MOST SACRED FAITH

But you, my friends, keep on building yourselves up on your most sacred faith. Pray in the power of the Holy Spirit, and keep yourselves in the love of God, as you wait for our Lord Jesus Christ in his mercy to give you eternal life.

JUDE 20–21 GNT

Would you consider your faith sacred? Is it a holy thing to you? Is it set apart from the other areas of your life?

Sometimes we get so caught up in the busyness of life that we forget how sacred our relationship with Jesus really is. It's a supernatural thing, a holy gift that the Creator of all would sweep down and embrace humanity. We can't treat it in glib fashion. It's a miracle, one that should leave us breathless and in awe.

Keep building yourself up in your faith. Remind yourself daily of its importance and magnificence. If you feel your faith slipping, go to God and ask Him to increase it. Live in this blessed faith, and do great things for Him.

It's a miracle, Jesus! I'll keep building myself up in my most holy faith, and I will see it for what it is—holy, supernatural, and a gift from You to help me navigate this life. Amen.

COME, LORD JESUS

He who gives his testimony to all this says, "Yes indeed!
I am coming soon!" So be it. Come, Lord Jesus!
REVELATION 22:20 GNT

Remember, as a child, how you waited for Daddy to come home from work at the end of the day? You couldn't wait to see him again, to throw yourself into his arms. You didn't have to wonder if he would show up. You knew he would. And the anticipation would have you so wound up, you could scarcely speak.

You can have that same assurance that Jesus, the one who died and rose again, is coming back to sweep you into His arms. The same Jesus who was in the beginning. The same Jesus who came as a babe in the manger. The same Jesus who clung to and died on the cross. The same Jesus who rose from the dead and ascended into heaven. The same Jesus who sent the Spirit to dwell inside all who believe.

Do you have a sense of anticipation about that? Daddy is coming home soon! And He can't wait to embrace you, His precious child.

I'm so ready for You to come, Jesus! So be
it! Come, Lord Jesus! Come! Amen.

SCRIPTURE INDEX

Old Testament

New Testament

ABOUT THE AUTHOR

Janice Thompson, who lives in the Houston area, writes romantic comedies, cozy mysteries, nonfiction devotionals, and musical comedies for the stage. She is the mother of four daughters and nine feisty grandchildren. When she's not writing books or taking care of foster dogs, you'll find her in the kitchen, baking up specialty cakes and cookies.